# THE CHUR
# GARDEN



Our Lady of Lourdes, Queen of Peace,
Rottingdean, Brighton

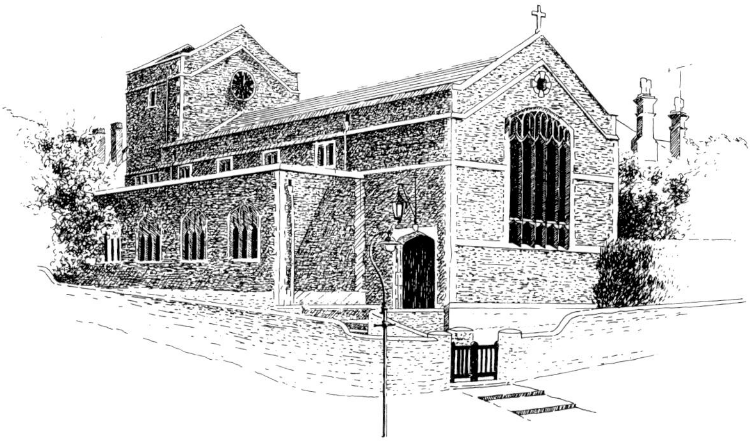

*The Church of Our Lady of Lourdes by Neal d'Enno*

Douglas d'Enno

By the same author:
*The Saltdean Story* (Phillimore, 1985)

First published in 2001 by DD Publishing
c/o 1 Bevendean Avenue
Saltdean, Brighton, East Sussex BN2 8LR
Tel.: 01273 882757/Fax: 01273 888590
E-mail:dougd@cwcom.net

The publisher acknowledges the financial support of the
Parish of Our Lady of Lourdes, Rottingdean,
and the Convent of St Martha, Falkirk, Stirlingshire



A CIP Record for this book is available from
the British Cataloguing in Publication Data Office



ISBN 0 9540033 0 6

Designed and typeset by CGB, Lewes
Printed by Tansleys the Printers
19 Broad Street, Seaford,
East Sussex, BN25 1LS

Dedicated to the people of the
parish – past, present
and future

In Thanksgiving

# Author's preface

In 1858 the Virgin Mary miraculously appeared, on numerous occasions, to young Bernadette Soubirous in Lourdes. One hundred years later, the centenary of these manifestations was commemorated in Rottingdean by the consecration of the church of Our Lady of Lourdes, Queen of Peace.

This fulfilled the dearest wish of the parish priest at the time, Father Patrick O'Brien, who for years had worked towards the goal of a Catholic church to serve the village and surrounding areas.

The building itself had been completed the year before. I well remember that time for it was in 1957 that I first moved from London to neighbouring Saltdean. From this coincidence, and the fact that my sister was married in Our Lady of Lourdes in March 1963, I felt (and feel) a close affinity with the church, an affinity which was to be strengthened in the early 1980s when compiling fairly detailed notes on the history of the building in connection with *The Saltdean Story*, published in 1985.

As I delved deeper into the background of the need for, and the construction of, the Church of Our Lady of Lourdes, I unearthed some fascinating details about the pioneering work carried out by a handful of nuns, who spoke virtually no English, in establishing first a chapel then a school for the burgeoning Catholic population in this locality and its environs.

I have provided as much detail as I could find about those early days and now, having been able to follow developments up to and including the Millennium year, I see an opportunity for the timely publication of the material I brought together nearly two decades ago. Certainly it is pleasing to know that the written and photographic records of the church's story, supplemented by valuable contributions from parishioners and others, showing developments over many decades have been preserved for future generations.

**Douglas d'Enno**
**Saltdean**
**January 2001**

# CONTENTS

## Part 1
## THE MAKING OF A PARISH



## Part 2
## A NEW CHURCH AND SCHOOL



*Front cover picture :* Our Lady of Lourdes church and the parish room.
*Back cover picture:* A rooftop view of the village of Rottingdean.

*Cover photos: Ron Fortune*

# Foreword

During the many years I served as Bishop of the Diocese of Arundel and Brighton, I made a number of visits to the delightful church of Our Lady of Lourdes in Rottingdean. I still clearly recollect some of the milestones in the church's growth to maturity which I was invited to celebrate with the parish, especially its Silver Jubilee in 1982, the opening of the parish room in 1993, the fortieth anniversary of the consecration in 1998 and the blessing of the Millennium Window in 2000. On each of these occasions, I was warmly welcomed by my fellow clergy and the parishioners.

This is a vibrant parish which has integrated well with the ancient village of which it forms part. In the space of less than 100 years, a Catholic community of several hundred souls, with a thriving primary school and a convent which has become a local landmark, have gradually appeared thanks to the pioneering work of a handful of nuns forced to flee their native France simply in order to follow their vocation unmolested.

Their efforts yielded abundant fruit and are recorded in detail in this unusual fusion of village chronicle and Catholic history.

**Cormac**
**Archbishop of Westminster**
November 2000

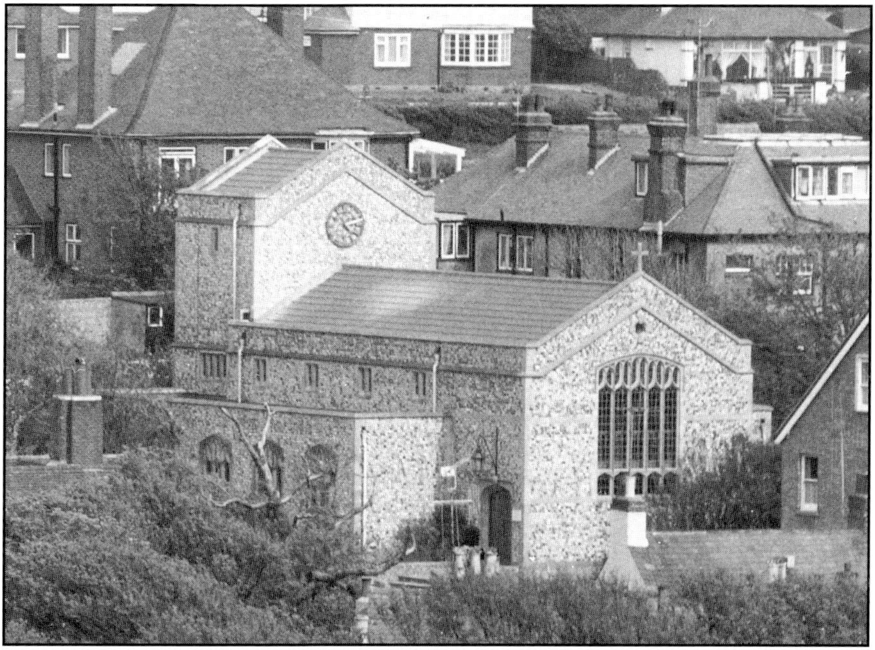

# 1

# Today and yesterday

NOT far from the pond in Rottingdean stands the Church of Our Lady of Lourdes, Queen of Peace. It was built in the modern Gothic style in 1957 with flint turned up by the plough in the surrounding fields. Flint was also used in the building of a nearby group of cottages, one of which, Bankside, is among the oldest dwellings in the village. The parish room attached to the church is screened by a hedge and fence and lies a few steps away from Eastfield, a solid, late Victorian house which serves as the presbytery.

The foundation of Rottingdean's flourishing Catholic population – Mass attendance averaged 392 in 2000 – was laid nearly one hundred years ago by the nuns of St Martha, whose convent is on the opposite side of The Green. Its history, and that of its forerunner which stood

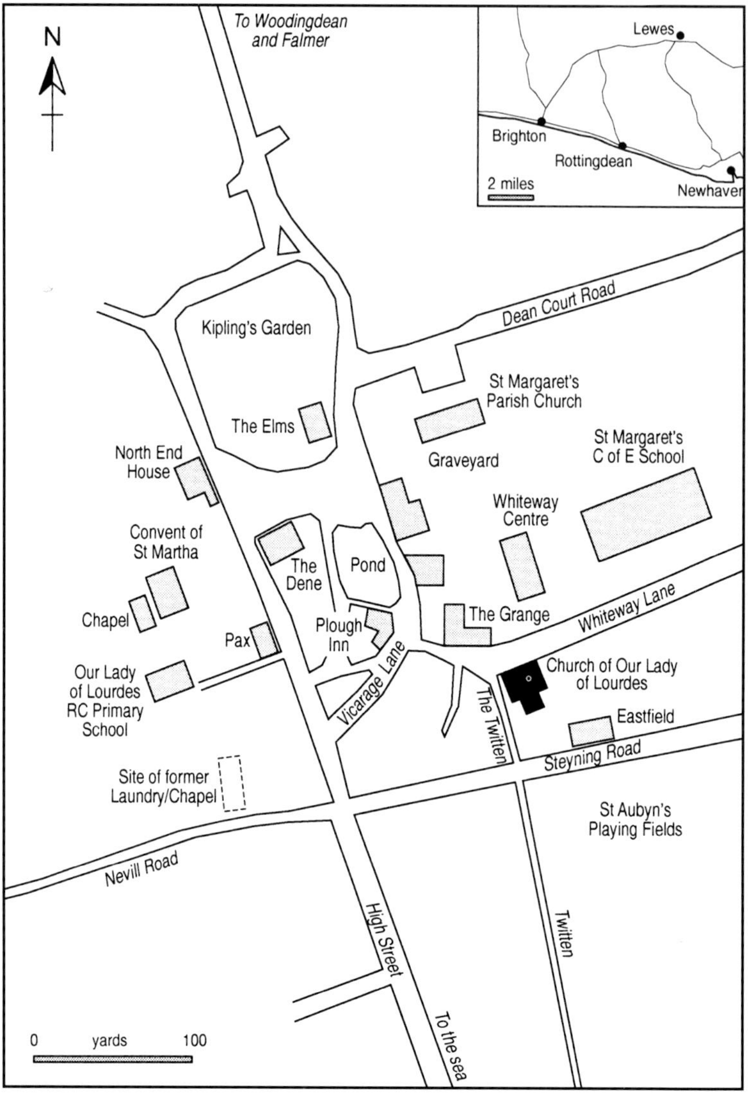


**Map showing selected sites in Rottingdean.**

near the sea, is the key to understanding the need to build the church of Our Lady of Lourdes.

It is necessary, therefore, to leave the village and travel to France where the seeds of Rottingdean's Catholic revival were sown.

## St Martha and her followers

The first steps in the foundation of the Order of the Sisters of St Martha were taken in Périgueux in 1643. Two young girls from Angoulême, Jeanne and Antoinette Juilhard, came forward to answer an appeal for help from the guardian of the poor at the Hôtel-Dieu Sainte Marthe and resolved to devote their lives to caring for the distressed and sick in the town. This was a time of religious wars, plagues and bad harvests and there was much work to be done.

The Juilhard sisters put all their energies into the Lord's service, receiving help from the priests of the mission, an institution founded by the Jesuits.

The bishop and the guardian of the poor placed the girls in charge of the hospital, under a contract which they accepted on the condition that lodgings were provided for the poor and an infirmary established for the sick. The girls were soon joined by many young people from Périgord.

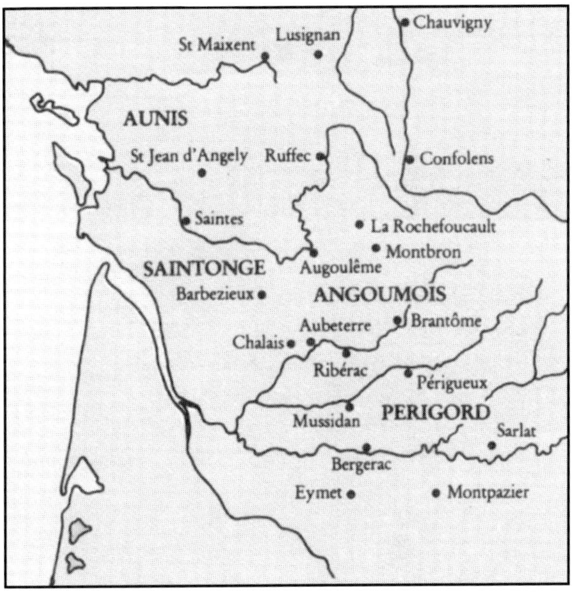


**Map showing the sites of the hospitals set up by the Sisters of St Martha in the seventeenth and eighteenth centuries**

At this time there was widespread distress in Angoulême, which had twice been ransacked by Protestant troops and its population decimated by the plague. The hot summer of 1645 was to exacerbate the situation. The hospital, Our Lady of the Angels, was finally built in *c*1650 and the Juilhard girls' cousin, Hélie Guillebauld, offered her help. The bishop placed her in charge of the establishment and she, like her cousins, was soon joined by many dedicated helpers.

The rules given to Hélie by the Jesuits were taken, in substance, from those of the Daughters of St Martha, as they had now become, in Périgueux. The project of the Order, which was submitted to the bishop, encompassed the vows of chastity and 'stability in the service of the poor'.

The Daughters of St Martha were influenced to a great degree by the charitable work of Vincent de Paul. He was one of six children of a poor peasant family in the Landes area who, in 1633, founded the Daughters of Charity. These were nuns without uniforms and without canonical status who made no solemn vows but had to live the three virtues of charity, humility and simplicity.

Eleven hospitals were opened in the seventeenth century by the Order of St Martha and a further fourteen in the eighteenth century. From them the nuns visited the sick and the downtrodden, and established schools and homes of refuge. They were so successful in their work for unfortunates that many affluent citizens looked to them for nursing care when they were sick and wanted their children to benefit from the good education provided by the sisters. Money paid for these services was used to subsidise the less fortunate.

**Edwige du Vivier, who became Mother Superior of the Sisters of St Martha.**

A third branch of the Order of St Martha, based at the town of Romans on the Drôme, was established in the early years of the nineteenth century. It was here that Edwige du Vivier had been born in 1785 in well-to-do circumstances. Her father was Counsellor to the Court at Grenoble and her mother related to François de Sales.

In 1812 the parish priest opened a school for young girls of poor families and the Bishop of Valence put Edwige in charge of teaching them. Two years later Romans, with its school, was destroyed by the Austrians. Edwige opened another school in another town and, at the request of the bishop, established a novitiate. When it was closed by Napoleon's soldiers she sought refuge in Vienne, coming back in July 1816 and calling her congregation the Sisters of St Martha.

Edwige du Vivier took the veil herself in September of that year and became Mother Superior of the Order she had founded, taking the name of Mother Marie Philippine.

## Early refugees from France

England has a history of receiving refugees from religious intolerance in France. During the French Revolution the stream of civil and religious refugees arriving in Brighton became a torrent after the September massacres of 1792. In October a party of thirty seven nuns driven out of their convent in Lille and with just £30 between them landed at Shoreham from the cross-Channel packet. The people of Brighton, learning of their plight, arranged for them to be brought to the town and accommodated at the New Ship Inn – which posed a problem for the proprietor as the nuns refused to sleep more than one to a bed, notwithstanding the ordeals they had suffered.

The Prince of Wales paid them a lengthy visit and subsequently opened a subscription for their relief. The sisters eventually made their way back to the continent via Dover and Brussels. In 1801 Napoleon Bonaparte ended the Revolution, signed a concordat with the papacy, and established the church as a religious agency supported by, and subservient to, the French state. This system lasted, with modifications, for a century, during monarchist, republican, and Bonapartist regimes.

## Anti-clerical conflict is revived

The emergence of the Third Republic in 1871 intensified the old conflict between clericals and anti-clericals. The victorious Republicans enacted a large amount of anti-clerical legislation. The Jesuits were suppressed and the laws of the Education Minister, Jules Ferry, were passed in 1880-1882. These established free, secular education and obligatory primary education; opened up secondary education for girls; made civil marriage

**The Mother House of the Sisters of St Martha at Le Bugue in the Dordogne in 1896.**

compulsory; and gave opportunities for divorce. From 1886, members of the clergy were forbidden to teach in the public schools and the Law of Association of 1901 suppressed nearly all the religious orders in France and confiscated their property. The anti-clerical Émile Combes, ironically a former seminarian, became Prime Minister of France in June 1902 and was in office until 1905. He dissolved as many as 135 different religious congregations, representing thousands of different houses. Convents, hospitals and schools were unjustly sequestrated.

These measures did not take place without protest. On 15 August 1902 some 15,000 people demonstrated against the closure of convent schools in Brittany. Nonetheless, on 18 March of the following year, the Government refused applications to teach from religious orders. On April 29 the dissolution of the French monasteries started. Soldiers on horseback moved in to a Chartreuse monastery high in the Alps to expel all the residents. Protests from the right, and the Chartreuse monks' own offer to pay two million francs to avoid expulsion, did not have any effect on the Government's determination to make any kind of religious teaching, even if it involved only one teacher in a school, subject to formal government authorisation. On 5 August a teachers' congress in Marseilles welcomed the abolition of religious instruction in schools.

In this troubled climate, expulsions of religious were numerous. Categorically refusing secularisation, or even partial secularisation, the Superiors of the Convent of St Martha at Le Bugue in the Dordogne, where there was a well-established school, determined to seek in a foreign country the religious freedom which France had denied them.

That country was England and the decision was a wise one.

In 1903, when Reverend Mother Emmanuel Parrot was Superior General of the Order, three of its members – Mother Jeanne de la Croix, the Assistant-General; Mother Estochie, the Bursar-General; and Sister Jeanne Thérèse who was to act as interpreter – left their native country to pave the way for a foundation.

They were going into the unknown but Divine Providence, and St Martha, were with them.

☆ ☆ ☆

## 2

# The seed becomes a flower

THE small advance party that arrived in England on 3 April 1903 to arrange accommodation for those of the Order who were to follow was welcomed by Francis Bourne, the Bishop of Southwark, the diocese which then included Sussex and Surrey. Negotiations were started at once to buy a house in Rottingdean and rent one at Hill View, High Barnet, Hertfordshire.

The deeds of sale of Bedgebury House at the seaward end of the High Street known as The Cliffe and later Manor Terrace, Rottingdean, were signed on 29 July 1903, the feast of St Martha, and the house was renamed Star of the Sea. In early August 1903, Mother Marguerite Marie Lajoumard, Superior of Le Bugue boarding school which had just been closed on government orders, sailed from France with five members of the community and their chaplain. They had a comfortable crossing to Newhaven. From her seat on deck Mother Marguerite Marie wrote in her diary:

> 'We can see the harbour – England is only a few miles away. May the Sacred Heart welcome us on our arrival. We offer Him ourselves to win over souls and we ask him to multiply the seed that St Martha is sowing today.'

On 13 August their chaplain, who knew England and its language, celebrated the first Mass in the convent's newly-opened chapel in the village. It was the first Catholic service to have taken place in Rottingdean for 300 years and Mother Marguerite wrote about it in a letter to Mother Emmanuel at Le Bugue:

> 'At eight o'clock your six religious were kneeling in front of the altar and

**The first resident sisters of the Order of St Martha at the Star of the Sea Convent – Sister Marguerite Marie (front row centre) the Superior and later Reverend Mother of the new convent. On her right is Sister St Félix. The others are Sisters Vitaline, Bénigne, St Paul, and Marie Eugène.**

the first Mass began. At this point I have to stop – there are feelings which cannot be described in any language. It is a hundredfold given by Jesus in return for a sacrifice one finds quite small compared with the great graces He gives us. Oh Mother, how we prayed for you, for the Congregation, and for France! During that first Elevation it was the prayer of Good Friday, for friends, for enemies, and for unbelievers. We were overcome with emotion during these prayers at the thought of Our Lord's generosity. What we have done is so little compared with what Our Lord has done for us. With the disciples of Emmaus we were able to say: "Stay with us, Lord."'

## Communities in exile

There had been a delay in the arrival of the sisters' luggage so before moving into Bedgebury House they spent a few days at the Convent of the Immaculate Heart of Mary in Newhaven which had been founded by another small group of nuns from France around 1900. For a time they occupied a house called Abbeville, which is still standing in Fort Road, and then moved to Meeching Place in Church Hill. This large house had, in addition to the buildings fronting the road, several small brick cottages and outhouses, tennis courts, a few acres of pasture for grazing cattle and a tree-lined walk. The convent school took in fee-paying pupils and boarders, with part of one of the buildings being used for 'lady boarders' paying for private accommodation. The nuns also taught in a non-fee-paying school in Newhaven and later at a school in Peacehaven.

During the Second World War the Newhaven convent sustained a direct hit in an air raid and one of the sisters was killed. Between 1940 and 1945 the Order occupied a nearby property which was sold after the war when the sisters moved to Billingshurst. The schools were taken over by the local authority and the East Sussex County Library Service acquired what had been the cloisters and the old chapel.

A number of other communities from France established thermselves along the coast. In September 1903, when he was appointed Archbishop of Westminster, Bishop Francis Bourne of the Southwark diocese gave the Sisters of Providence of Rouen a substantial holiday home he had acquired in Seaford and which he had named Annecy after his patron, St Francis of Sales. At that time Seaford's Catholic population totalled only five or six. The French Augustinian Fathers of Newhaven took over as chaplains to the sisters and offered daily Mass in the chapel, which served the parish until the opening of the church of St Thomas More in 1936. Today average Mass attendance there is 434.

(*The author remembers the Annecy chapel well. When a five year old boarder he almost set fire to the sanctuary carpet during Benediction by mishandling the thurible.*)

To the west, in Brighton, the same scenario of a handful of pioneering French nuns making their way to these shores was played out in that summer of 1903. Seeking asylum for the Sisters of Charity and Christian Instruction of Nevers, whose schools were being closed, the city's bishop had written to Bishop Bourne, who invited the Sisters to the parish of St Joseph, Brighton. The first two were welcomed by the nuns of the Blessed Sacrament Convent, Kemp Town. With the rector's help, they moved into a house in Wellington Road, where they were joined by other members of the community. The nuns from France took over the care of the sacristy of St Joseph, visited the poor and the sick and opened a school. In September a further contingent of exiles arrived and a second foundation was set up at Tonbridge in Kent. The following year the sisters established a convent, school and chapel in Withdean, under the patronage of Our Lady of Lourdes. On the patronal feast day in 1910, the money to build a church was promised by a wealthy Irishwoman, Mrs Catherine Broderick, who financed no fewer than nine Catholic churches, including those at Herne Bay, the seminary chapel at Wonersh and the chapel of the Little Sisters of the Poor in Hove. The church that was built is St Mary's, Preston Park, where average mass attendance today is 440, triple the number of the earliest congregation.

When Catholic schools in Brighton were reorganised in the early 1970s, Lourdes Convent was closed and became part of Cardinal Newman School. The buildings, including the chapel which had been rebuilt in 1938 in elaborate Gothic style by J S Gilbert, were demolished in 1972, leaving the original school building, Grove Lodge, to continue as St Bernadette's RC Middle School a year later.

## The village at the turn of the century

The Rottingdean to which those first nuns came was in many ways very different from what it is today. South of the crossroads the High Street was much narrower. Where the bus shelter stood until recently was a large flint-walled property called West House. On the Brighton road next to the garden of West House were two cottages, and next to them was Field Cottage, formerly a threepence-a-week school. They were all demolished when the road was widened in the 1930s.

The White Horse opened in 1603 and was to become one of the busiest coaching inns on the Brighton to Dover Road. It had stabling for forty horses and in 1820 a new coach, the Royal Charlotte, was introduced. It could do the Dover run in ten hours.

Stephen Welfare, a later proprietor, continued the inn's transport tradition by pioneering a horse bus mail and passenger service to Brighton. The green in front of the old inn, which was replaced by the present White Horse Hotel in 1934, became known as Welfare's Green. Three houses stood on the clifftop fields, two near the road and the third on the cliff edge. The latter was approached by a road which ran

**The old White Horse Hotel and, centre, the Star of the Sea convent with its impressive pillared portico.**

**July 1904 – and passengers from a horse bus drawn up in front of the White Horse Hotel make their way past the Star of the Sea to the High Street.**

along the cliff top, but one day the road and the house it served fell into the sea.

Manor Terrace, formerly The Cliffe, took its name from the three-storey property called Manor House which stood on the south-east corner of the crossroads and which ended its days as a branch of Barclay's Bank. Behind it was Manor Cottage where the Taylor family lived for four years when they first came to Rottingdean from Newmarket in 1919. It was only yards away from the Star of the Sea convent, which Jillisen Taylor, then a non-Catholic, attended from the age of four until she was eight. Jillisen is now Sister Marie-Christine of Lourdes, Brighton. She belongs to the Sisters of Charity of Nevers, the Order that Bernadette joined – indeed, the saint's incorrupt body lies at the Mother House.

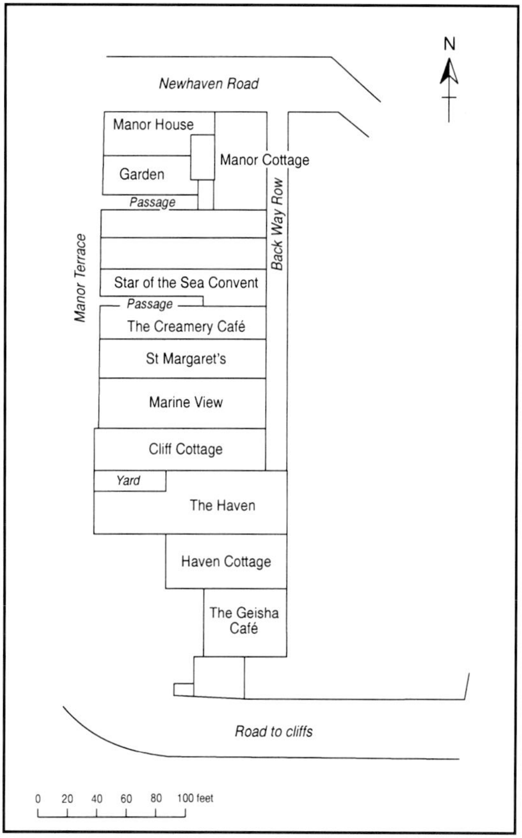


**Properties on the east side of Manor Terrace.**

On the seaward side of the original garden of Manor Cottage stood five three-storey, double-fronted houses, some with wooden railings and some with iron ones, which little boys would beat as they passed with their iron hoop-sticks. Bedgebury House had a distinctive portico, making it stand out from the other houses in the terrace. Next door to it was a creamery and this was the name given to the property when it became a tea shop. Early owners of The Creamery included the Misses Lively, a Mrs Hazeldean from the old White Horse, and later still Miss Cuttress. It is now called

The Coach House. To the south of the original five large houses stood a huddle of dwellings, among them Cliff Cottage; The Haven which had an odd, tiny cottage attached to it; and the shed-like Geisha, a restaurant, tea room and dance hall. This complex of buildings was demolished when Highcliff Court was built in 1967.

## Two families of the faith

There were just two Catholic families in the village at the turn of the last century – the Furlongs and the Hennessys.

Arthur Eavington Ridsdale in his *Annals of Old Rottingdean*, written jointly with his sister, Lucy, who married three times Prime Minister Stanley Baldwin, gave both the 'village' name and the true name of the Irish Catholic family that lived in the area behind West Street and the High Street known as Golden Square.

> 'In Golden Square there lived a family called Murphy – their real name was Furlong, but as they were Irish they were known as Murphy. Jimmy

**Golden Square was behind the north side of West Street. The old houses were demolished in the 1930s.**

> Murphy used to help me as a boy because he was a great hand at ratcatching and always sent me word when a likely stack was to be thrashed'.

James Furlong and his wife Johanna had moved to the village around 1886, although they had been in England for more than a decade, having been married in 1875 in the Roman Catholic Chapel in Folkestone. They had left Ireland a short time previously. Johanna was a labourer's daughter and James was a private in the 41st Foot, the Welch Regiment, based at Shorncliffe, the military barracks in the west part of Folkestone. His father, John, was a river pilot.

Novelist Angela Thirkell, who had a limited but loyal following for her individualistic tales of family dramas in country house settings, as a child often spent summer holidays at Rottingdean in the rambling old house belonging to her grandparents, Sir Edward and Lady Georgiana Burne-Jones. She also used the Furlong family's 'village' name when she wrote, in *Three Houses,* published in 1931, that:

> 'Mr Murphy, the head of one Irish family, was blind of an eye, and was held up to us as an awful warning because his trade was stone-breaking and he would not wear glasses to protect his eyes and one day a splinter flew into his eye and he was blind to this day. Where exactly the moral came in I don't know, as our opportunities for stone-breaking were practically non-existent; but it impressed us very much.'

Johanna Furlong is listed as the occupant of 4, Golden Square under her 'village' name of Murphy in *Pike's Local Directory* of 1910 and is also in the 1926 edition as 'Mrs J Murphy.' James and Johanna are buried together in Rottingdean churchyard. The inscriptions at the head and foot of their grave read respectively:

OF YOUR CHARITY PRAY FOR THEIR SOULS.
THEE ALSO HE HATH MADE TO SEE THE LIGHT OF HEAVEN.

The couple had five children – Michael, Nicholas, Theresa, Hanna Statia and Mary. A sixth, John, was born in 1877 but died when three months old. Michael, who was born in Rottingdean in 1879, worked with horses at The Paddock in what is now Gorham Avenue. He was subsequently employed by Hall's, a manufacturing company. His daughter, Nora Susan Johanna, born in St Leonards in 1911, also worked for Hall's, where she was a secretary for forty years. When she died in a nursing home in Dartford, Kent, on 23 December 1998 the family name of Furlong died with her.

There were some lively local characters in the 'Murphy'/Furlong family, or connected to it by marriage. Nora's sister, Theresa, married twice, first to one Percival Loader, by whom she had three daughters, and then to George Alexander Adkins, her mother's lodger and the local barber. He came from Newhaven and was the first to employ the eminent local author and folksinger, Bob Copper. One of Bob's duties was to take used towels from the barber's shop in a small cottage called The Nest to Theresa's cottage for laundering and return with clean ones.

Bob, in one of his books, recalls that when at work Barber Adkins, who was nicknamed 'Porky', spurned small talk and gossip and entertained his often bewildered clients with non-stop dissertations on matters of political, historical or religious interest.

The eldest Furlong daughter, Mary Elisabeth Oloysion, married Robert Gibson Young in London on 16 May 1910. He was a jockey who had been apprenticed to John Hornsby at Wantage in Berkshire, trainer of the once famous horse Victor Wild, and he went on to win a number of races in this country and South Africa.

**Robert and Mary Young with sons Leo and Bob.**

In the First World War Robert, a non-Catholic Scotsman, served in France and Belgium with the Royal Army Veterinary Corps, attending to the horses he had always loved. He later became a Catholic and when he died in 1962, at the age of seventy five, his funeral service was held at Our Lady of Lourdes church where he had been a helper in many ways for a number of years.

Two sons were born of this marriage. William, usually known

by his middle name, Leo, but nicknamed 'Lebby', and Robert, who settled in Queensland, Australia and died there some years ago. Leo had a distinguished war record, serving with the BEF in 1940 and the Airborne Forces Developing Centre in 1944. His wedding on 18 September 1937 to Florence Edith Little at St Martha's Convent was only the second to be held there.

The daughter of Leo and Florence is Mrs (Mary) Jean Harvey who was at the Convent of St Martha from 1949 to 1960, where she was known to the sisters and school friends as 'Mary-Jean'. She was married at Our Lady of Lourdes in 1966 and lives just off the Falmer Road, Rottingdean, with her husband, John. One of their two sons, Andrew, a postgraduate student at Sussex University, has continued the family link with Our Lady of Lourdes, being an altar server there for nearly twenty years. His brother Nicholas, an airline pilot now living at Richmond, was also a server there for more than a decade.

## The Hennessys

Coastguard David Hennessey, born in Ballycotton, County Cork in 1842, had seen service at Selsey and Hythe before he was transferred to take charge of the coastguard station at Rottingdean in the 1890s. He moved with his wife, Honoria, and their eight children into Field Cottage on the coast road.

The story of the family's early days in Rottingdean is told by granddaughter Isabelle McHardy, neé Sandever, the first bride to be married at the Convent of St Martha, in *The Coming to Rottingdean of the Hennessy Family,* which she wrote in 1977. They arrived by land and by sea:

> '. . . my mother, Kathleen, was about six years of age and it would have been about the year 1890. The majority of the family, together with furniture etc. travelled by cutter . . . only grandmother with the three youngest, Aileen, Charles and Ivan, travelling overland by train. All luggage, furniture etc. was manhandled up from the beach to the house they were to occupy. . .
>
> 'At that time there was no Catholic church in the village and every Sunday morning grandmother would get all the children ready and grandfather would walk with them to St John the Baptist church in Kemp Town, there being no means of transport. They would all go fasting as in

The Hennessey family. Back row: William and Mary. Second row: Charles, Honoria, David Snr and James. Far left is David, far right Kathleen. Aileen is seated left foreground and Ivan is on his mother's lap.

Rottingdean's coastguard cottages, long since demolished, were on the site of the present car park.

those days Catholics could only receive Holy Communion if they had fasted from midnight.

'After Mass and Holy Communion the family would be invited into the convent next door to the church for a cup of tea before making their homeward journey which, weather permitting, they would make by way of the Daddy Longlegs transport, a sort of railway carriage on long legs which ran out to sea between Kemp Town and Rottingdean, but which frequently broke down.'

This was the Brighton and Rottingdean Seashore Electric Railway, designed and operated by Magnus Volk. It opened on 29 November 1896 and was almost totally destroyed a week later by the great gale which finished off the already unsteady Chain Pier. It re-opened in late August 1897. Its car, which was officially named *The Pioneer,* could accommodate 150 passengers and took thirty five minutes to travel from the Banjo Groyne at the bottom of Paston Place to the pier at Rottingdean.

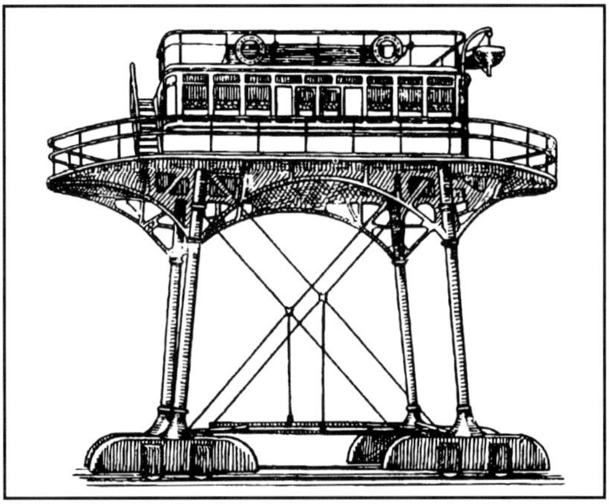

**The 'Daddy Longlegs transport'.**

Of the couple's three daughters, Mary Elizabeth married Charles French and died in 1937 at the age of fifty eight. Her sister, Aileen, affectionately known as 'Nin', in her later years ran a small wool and haberdashery shop in Rottingdean High Street. She died in 1972, aged eighty two.

On 29 November 1909, the third daughter, Kathleen, was married to Albert Sandever at St John the Baptist, Kemp Town. She was in service and he was head lad at McKay's racing stables to the rear of North End House, Rottingdean.

Albert started a riding school in stables of his own just north of North End House, later moving his horses down to stables next to the White Horse Hotel, facing the sea. In the 1930s, when that was about to be demolished, he moved his school to some farm buildings just south of the bowling green – now known as Challenor's Mews – where he remained until the outbreak of the war. The two Sandever daughters were born in the village, Honoria Sarah, nicknamed 'Nonie', in 1910, and Mary Isabella in 1913.

Their first home was 5 Vicarage Terrace, an old cottage within yards of the present Church of Our Lady of Lourdes. During the First World War, the Sandever family moved into Field Cottage, and David and Honoria, whose children had by then grown up, took over the Vicarage Terrace cottage. Of the five Hennessy sons William, who was born at Aldwick in 1880, was toll keeper at Shoreham's toll bridge and retired to a converted railway carriage on Shoreham Beach. His son, David, became a priest against his advice and for a time served as chaplain with Barnum and Bailey's Circus in the USA. When World War Two broke out David was caught in France and directed to 'walk home'.

**Field Cottage, in which the Hennessys were succeeded by the Sandevers. It was demolished in 1933.**

He must have done so successfully for in December 1940 Rottingdean's priest-in-charge, Father James Austin, was seeking the bishop's permission for a newly-ordained priest to say mass in a private house. His letter explains the reasons for the request, which was granted:

'David Hennessy will be ordained for the Assumptionist Fathers at Hitchin on the 21st December 1940. His home is at Newhaven. He wishes to obtain the privilege of celebrating one of his first masses at the home of his grandmother in Rottingdean. She is an old lady of 84 years, a fervent Catholic, but unable to get to mass. The opportunity provided may be her only chance of hearing mass again.

'The additional reason is also cogent. She has been looking forward to the ordination of this priest in the family for a long time, and would greatly appreciate being able to assist at his mass. A further plea may be advanced on the grounds that the Hennessys are one of the first and the oldest Catholic family in Rottingdean and by their charity have helped in the establishment of the faith in this village.'

Father David Hennessy died in October 1982. The first job his uncle, David Richard Hennessy, had was with horse bus operator Fred Thomas, for whom he drove carriages and other horse-drawn vehicles. He then worked as a taxi-driver for Fred's son, George, whose brother Charles, ran what was believed to be the first purpose-built garage in the country which their father had built in West Street, Rottingdean in 1896.

**Father David Hennessy and his grandmother, Honoria.**

Charles put this garage on the motoring map by becoming one of the first men to travel round the world in a motor car.

He was the co-driver with American millionaire, Charles Glidden, on a 33,600 mile journey which took them to thirty five countries in 271 days. Nor was this Charles Thomas's first long distance drive. In 1902, at the age of nineteen, he took the first car to India, delivering a Napier to the Maharajah of Balrampur. Three years later he won the first International Motor Boat Race from Folkestone to Boulogne in Lord Howard de Walden's Napier-powered speedboat.

David Hennessy took up with the Thomases again after the 1914-18 war, during which he had served abroad on transport service. He then started a taxi business of his own in premises on the Brighton Road. Like his father before him, he was a very able fisherman and had his own boat which he kept on the beach.

David's brother, James Austin Hennessy, was the black sheep of the family – a brash, fun-loving salesman for a motor company in London who would come down to Sussex at weekends in all kinds of fancy vehicles, always out to impress.

The two youngest brothers, Charles Stideford and Ivan Thomas, were casualties of the First World War. Charles was killed in action on the Somme on 25 February 1917 at the age of twenty eight, while Ivan was killed in action on HMS *Good Hope* off Coronel on 1 November 1914, aged twenty one. Their names and details are inscribed on a headstone in St Margaret's churchyard.

☆ ☆ ☆

# 3

# The Star of the Sea

THE sisters, one of whom could speak a little English, quickly had Bedgebury House adapted to their needs and opened it to the world as the Star of the Sea.

The convent was blessed by l'Abbé Veyssière, a professor from St Joseph's (Boys') College, Périgueux, who stayed in the village for two months in 1903. Another priest from the same college, l'Abbé Ravel, was chaplain in 1907-08.

**L'Abbé Veyssière and, below, l'Abbé Ravel.**

The occasion was one of great delight to the Hennessey family for it meant that there would be Mass in the convent every Sunday and they would no longer have to walk the four miles to church in Kemp Town. It is said that David Hennessy, who had taken the nuns under his wing and provided all kinds of practical help, fell down on his knees in the road in humility and gratitude when Honoria handed over the keys of the building.

After much preparatory work, a small oratory was set up. The first twelve chairs bought for it cost five shillings each but were to prove good value, for they gave at least fifty years' service in one location or another. Brighton parishioners helped to furnish the chapel, the Sisters of Mercy gave a vestment; the Children of Mercy made one; and the Sacred Heart Sisters donated a cope.

To support themselves the French sisters took in 'lady boarders' and taught French, music and fine sewing. They were very gifted and the programmes, feast-day cards, almanacs, tiny booklets of art and verse and small pictures, each one drawn and hand-painted, are miniature works of art. They also produced a book of 188 French hymns, each one carefully transcribed in copy book writing.

**A decorative prayer card produced by the sisters.**

## Language problems

As well as earning their living and fulfilling their daily office, the nuns visited and offered comfort to the sick of the village. Shopping was quite a daunting challenge for them at first, with all kinds of linguistic confusions arising, to the amusement of the shopkeepers.

The school started with only a few pupils but the numbers soon grew. Lady Katharine Gordon, who came to Rottingdean in 1905, was among the first and her memories of those days were happy ones:

> 'I was overjoyed when it transpired that instead of returning to boarding school I was to be allowed to remain here for one term in order to be with my elder sister during the short period before her marriage. For that one term, I attended in the mornings the Star of the Sea Convent which was close to the spot where St Margaret's flats now stand – conveniently near the beach – to which I occasionally repaired in preference to school. It added much to my enjoyment that the nuns, who had only recently arrived from France, could not speak English. I taught them a lot.'

Another pupil at the convent school was Reginald Coen who lived in a house in the High Street called Glenmore from 1903-1912. His father was the postmaster and when he died his mother, Eleanor, became postmistress. Reginald did not go on to the village National School because of ill-health. He was educated at home by a nurse and governess, Miss Ethel Smithers, who later married and in 1917, as Mrs Bowles, also became Rottingdean's postmistress – a position from which she retired in 1964 at the age of eighty four.

**This postcard of the convent – its portico is just left of the car – is postmarked May 1919. It was sent by Sister Anne-Louise to Miss J Seymour in Brighton and bears the message: 'I shall be glad if you would come tomorrow for drawing at 3 o'clock'.**

The language problems of the French sisters, the convent buildings and their schooldays there are also remembered with affection, and in happy detail, by Isabelle McHardy (née Sandever), her sister Nonie, their cousin, Kathleen Willson, and Mrs Laura Jepson (née Thomas).

Isabelle's and Nonie's Auntie Nin was about thirteen when the nuns first came to the village and she was among the first pupils. Two of her younger brothers, Charles and Ivan, 'were always running in and out of the building – and that was before they were even pupils there. They had a lovely time and often talked to the nuns, who were clearly very well-disposed towards them'.

Isabelle was very happy there – 'I loved my schooldays – it was great.' She made her First Communion in the little chapel with three other pupils:

> 'I think we were more excited about our lovely white dresses and veils with a wreath of roses than we were taking in the significance of the day. We were also allowed to wear all our finery for Benediction in the evening'.

Her sister, Nonie, first attended the convent at the age of three in

1913. She recalls 'crying and screaming her way down the High Street,' escorted by a big girl, Dorothy Smith, the daughter of the licensee of the Plough Inn. In common with most of the pupils, she was somewhat in awe of the Reverend Mother. Nonie learned arithmetic, writing and French and did well in her lessons, entering for an examination when aged about ten. The convent did not then take pupils above that age as it did not have suitable facilities for them, so she was sent as a boarder, with her sister Isabelle, to the school run by the Sisters of St Martha in Barnet, North London.

Her cousin, Kathleen, remembers chanting 'I'm going to school tomorrow, I'm going to school tomorrow, I'm so happy', as she walked with her mother along what is now Whiteway Lane.

'When it was wet and windy my mother would take me to the school. We went up the alleyway by The Creamery and there was a horrible dog there that used to bark at us. We went in this funny little door and as we got in the door there was a place where we hung our coats. If you went in through the front door, the little chapel was on the left and on the right was a room where they used to give music lessons. One schoolteacher was a Miss Clark. There was also a lay teacher called Rosemary – I can see her now. She was tall with dark curly hair. She taught us writing and reading. We all had slates. There weren't many children. They had a couple of actresses' children there – one was called Popsy, I can't remember the other one but she was the daughter of a well-known actresss*. There was this great big room in which we did everything . . . We did dumb-bells and clubs and ribbon dances. And learning. I never did go upstairs – they only had the one classroom and that was downstairs. It was a boarding school then and after a time – I suppose I must have been about six or seven – I had to go to the village school . . . '

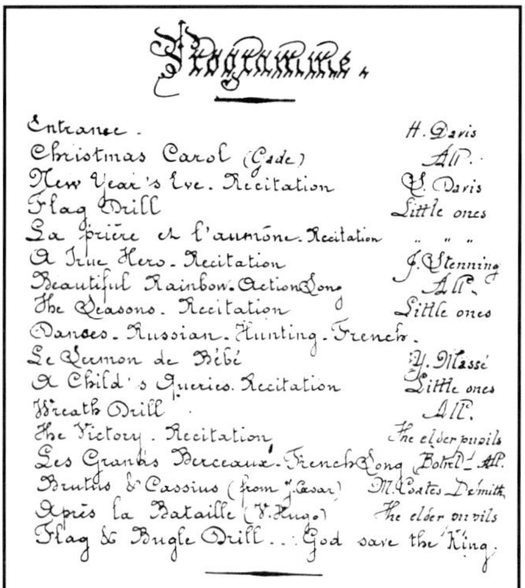
Programme.

| | |
|---|---|
| Entrance. | H. Davis |
| Christmas Carol (Gade) | All. |
| New Year's Eve. Recitation | E. Davis |
| Flag Drill | Little ones |
| La prière et l'aumône. Recitation | " " " |
| A True Hero. Recitation | J. Stenning |
| Beautiful Rainbow. Action Song | All. |
| The Seasons. Recitation | Little ones |
| Dances. Russian. Hunting. French. | |
| Le Sermon de Bébé | Y. Massé |
| A Child's Queries. Recitation | Little ones |
| Wreath Drill | All. |
| The Victory. Recitation | The elder pupils |
| Les Grands Berceaux. French Song (Botrel) | All. |
| Brutus & Cassius (from J. Caesar) | M. Coates. D. Smith |
| Après la Bataille (V. Hugo) | The elder pupils |
| Flag & Bugle Drill . . . God save the King. | |

Xmas, 1914.

**The 1914 Christmas concert programme.**

* The well-known actress was Fay Compton for whom James Barrie wrote *Peter Pan*.

School was from 9am to 12 noon and from 2pm to 4pm except on Wednesdays and Saturdays when it was mornings only. The sister who taught Kathleen was very strict about reading and spelling – any word mis-spelt had to be written out twenty times. She was allowed to spend some time with the boarders and as a member of the choir she sang the Mass in Latin and, as Christmas approached, they practised carols. At the end of term the pupils would give a concert of singing, poetry and ribbon dancing for the Reverend Mother and the nuns and each child would be given two sweets when it was over.

Kathleen made her First Communion on 16 July 1922, the Feast of Our Lady of Mount Carmel, spending her Communion day with the boarders, and she was subsequently confirmed at St John the Baptist, Kemp Town. On Sundays she would be taken to eight o'clock Mass but as she was prone to fainting and might thus be unable to receive Communion, the priest kindly decided to administer it before Mass.

Laura Jepson, who now lives in Denton, is the daughter of pioneer round-the-world motorist, Charles Thomas. She attended the convent for the best part of a decade and among her fellow pupils was her cousin Iris Thomas; Lucy and Winnie Hilder, daughters of the butcher; their cousin, Gladys Hilder, whose father was one of the two village bakers; and the O'Connell girls from the fish shop.

Like Kathleen Willson, she recalls approaching the convent along the side passage of The Creamery:

> ' . . . At the back of the house was a very large room looking onto a lovely garden. And we all were together there. I remember Lucy – and Winnie, [the model for Velvet, the part played by Elizabeth Taylor in the film of Enid Bagnold's *National Velvet*] – but we didn't see her very often. She'd be seen riding her pony quite a lot. A girl called Marion Howell went there later on. I do remember one litle crippled girl. She lived with the Snuddens. George Snudden's daughter, Hetty, used to look after her. I think she must have had polio or something, She was quite helpless. We all took care of her.
>
> 'I remember the nuns at the old convent. They were lovely. There was Sister St Patrick especially. The little chapel on the left was quite small but very nice. I often used to go to Benediction there. Then we had a music teacher called Miss Clark – she used to teach me the piano. The room on the right was where I was taught music. We were taught how to behave. We did have a few little boys at one period but I think they got a bit much. There were three or four – I think one of my brothers was there for

a little while. I expect it was Dudley because he was the eldest brother. . . Of course we had boarders there as well. . . about half a dozen or so. They came from away somewhere.

'Latterly, before I left, the sisters had another house near the Star of the Sea. They had some classrooms in there and I went there. That was towards the end of my time there, about 1923. I think they took it because they had too many pupils and wanted to expand. It was a tall house about two above the convent towards the crossroads. But the boarders still stayed at the Star of the Sea'.

Laura was awarded a Certificate of Merit for arithmetic, French and general progress and a prize for good work and singing. She left the covent when she was thirteen and after a spell at the village school and secretarial training she went on to become secretary to Brighton's Borough Treasurer.

## France severs links with the Vatican

While the convent and its little school were becoming established in England, anti-clericalism continued unabated across the Channel. On 29 July 1904 France severed links with the Vatican and on 9 December 1905 the Law of Separation sundering Church and State was enacted. The following February, 570 people were injured in riots as Government officials started to make an inventory of property owned by the Church. The new law guaranteed freedom of religion but it imposed severe restrictions on religious education and the ownership of property. It was denounced by Pope Pius X. 'We pray to God that the enemies of religion will stop persecuting us,' he declared. 'We shall fight hate with love, fallacy with truth and intimidation and humiliation with forgiveness.' His denunciation of the Government for trying to destroy the country's religious faith followed the failure of attempts by French church leaders to contest the Law of Separation. In August he protested to French bishops against the secularisation of France and in December told French priests to remain in their churches until driven out.

A law requiring church services to be registered as public meetings came into effect on 13 December and police served notices on the clergy who failed to comply with it. The services went on, but sixty nine priests who defied the order were charged. The Papal Agent was also expelled from France.

On 2 January 1907, a law came into force banning the crucifix from schools. Little wonder that, on 11 January, Pope Pius should claim that French government policies were aimed at 'de-christianising' France and on April 15 he officially condemned the separation of the French Church and State. Anti-clerical ideas and methods spread from France and were adopted, in varying ways, in other Latin countries. In Switzerland a Government decision was taken on 30 June 1907 to split the Church and State, despite a national referendum on 20 January in which the voting was against such a measure.

## Peace and calm in England

In England there was no such disharmony. All was tranquil in Rottingdean and the nuns followed their peaceful and charitable vocations unmolested. Some insight into the state of affairs at the Star of the Sea can be gleaned from a letter, dated 25 June 1912, written in not very fluent English, by the convent secretary, in the absence of the Reverend Mother, to an unnamed member of the clergy:

**An embroidery class in peaceful progress.**

'Our little Mission is very poor in details: it was opened in August 1903 when we were expelled from France; we had two children baptised at Christmas of the same year; last year also another baptism of an Adult in August and a little number of First Communions, four or five I think. Not many pupils in the moment, ten Protestant ones, from the village and two Catholic Destitute Girls we bring up. The Children are all behaving like Catholic ones (saying the same prayers when at school and learning Catechism and Bible). Only three small Catholic families, some servants; in summer, lot of visitors; Families are received in a house belonging to the Convent for holidays; the Xaverian Brothers from Clapham come down every year, also, for their summer holidays. Have two Masses on Sundays, during summer.

> Exposition of the Bl. Sacrament four hours, every first Sunday in the year. I enclose a Post Card representing our dear little Chapel, the half only is seen; on each side of the Altar, Our Lady of Lourdes and the Sacred Heart, St Martha over the Chimney (our Holy Patron), St Joseph lower, on the opposite side . . . Of course, we have a resident French Chaplain and Mass every day. Benediction Sundays and Thursdays.'

To make ends meet the sisters catered for visitors during the summer and Christmas holidays. The weekly tariff for 1913 was six shillings (30p) for ladies and seven shillings (35p) for gentlemen. Meals were included but light was sixpence (2½p) and shoe polishing a penny extra.

## Xaverians at West House

When members of the Xaverians – a male teaching order from Clapham where a college had been opened in 1897– made their annual holiday visits to Rottingdean they stayed at West House which they had purchased some time before the First World War. As a temporary measure until more suitable premises could be found, they opened a *juvenate* or novitiate of their Order there in 1918. Previously, novices had been trained in one or other of the school communities in England,

**West House (centre) has a large board on its northern elevation advertising the White Horse Hotel behind it.**

namely Mayfield, Clapham, Manchester and Attree Villa in Brighton which had been a Xaverian College since 1909.

Among the first novices at Rottingdean was Cyril Norris who arrived from London in November, just after Armistice Day, and was almost immediately struck down by the Spanish influenza which was claiming so many young lives at that time. He was permitted to take his vows on his deathbed on 1 December 1918, choosing the name Brother Francis Xavier. He died the following day and was buried in Rottingdean churchyard. Notes left to the Rottingdean Preservation Society by Mrs Marie-Thérèse Magee, née Achard, who came to the village with her mother in 1917, mention the school on the West House site, and the 'flu epidemic which caused Cyril Norris's tragic death:

> 'Several large houses opposite the Convent housed Christian Brothers, with pupils (boarders), for several years. Some died of 'flu in 1918.'

The *Brighton Catholic Magazine* had a hearty welcome for the Xaverians:

> 'The arrival in our midst of two Xaverian Brothers and of their postulants brings the Catholic Community of Rottingdean to seventy, a respectable number, and a force which emphasizes our urgent need of a larger place of worship for the Sunday Services at least. . . Here in England alone, Catholics owe the Xaverian Brothers a great debt of gratitude. They have been particularly hard hit by the war. Their long years of patient and very successful toil in Belgium have been jeopardised by the German invasion and occupation. The ranks of their gallant army of Brothers have been thinned out. Their once prosperous Novitiate in Belgium is closed. It is, therefore, of vital importance to the life of this hitherto flourishing congregation, that the depleted ranks be filled up by other equally generous youths ready to follow in the noble footsteps of their valiant forerunners. Hence the opening of the Novitiate at Rottingdean – May God bless this new venture for Christ and for souls. May it prove a fervent nursery of true Xaverian aspirants, full of the generous and noble spirit of the Saintly Founder of the Institute.'

Eighteen months after it opened the novitiate was transferred to Deeping St James, near Peterborough, and the property it had occupied was sold shortly afterwards.

In its February 1918 issue, the *Brighton Catholic Magazine* brought the story of St Martha's convent up to date for its readers:

> 'Our Lady, Star of the Sea – The title would suit a church of no mean dimensions. As it is, however, the fifty resident Catholics of Rottingdean

**The convent oratory**

cannot as yet boast of church or chapel of their own and they are indeed grateful to the French Community of the Sisters of St. Martha's Convent for the privilege of being able to hear Holy Mass and attend the liturgical services in their little oratory . . . The Sisters have a small school for little girls and boys – thirty pupils in all – besides this day school, the Sisters also receive lady-boarders. The Community has had a struggling existence during the past fifteen years, but in their silent way the good sisters have undoubtedly done much good work both by opening a temporary Home to our Blessed Lord, with an Altar wherein the Holy Sacrifice of the Mass is daily offered, and by being the means of lessening prejudice against the Catholic Church.'

## Services, devotions and plans for expansion

Anyone wishing to attend services at the convent oratory, certainly in 1918, would have had to watch out for announcements and keep a carefully annotated diary, since the stated times of worship changed almost monthly.

Mass on Sundays was held in February, with sermon, at 8am and on Palm Sunday in March at 7.30am. No announcement of times of services was given in the April issue of the *Brighton Catholic Magazine.* By May there was a Low Mass at 7.30am and a Sung Mass at 10am, although the following month the Low Mass time changed to 8am. These two times remained in force until October and presumably beyond. Weekday masses during the period were held at 8am from February to May then at 7.15am from June to September inclusive, reverting to 7.30am in October.

Benediction was held on Thursdays at 4pm in February but was replaced the following month by Special Devotions and Instruction every evening at 8pm. By May Benediction, with sermon and rosary, was at 6pm and in June this time also applied but was split into sermon, rosary and Benediction on days other than Thursdays, and a service on Fridays which did not include a sermon. In October the time changed to 5.pm and the service was held 'every Thursday and Days of Devotion.'

Confessions were heard (in English and French) at 4.30pm on Thursdays and 5pm on Saturdays during February and any day after Benediction in May; similarly in June, with the addition of Saturdays at 6pm; Thursdays and Saturdays at 6pm in July; and from 5pm on Saturdays from August to October.

Saturday 16 February 1918 was a red letter day for Rottingdean Catholics. For the first time, they were privileged to have the Forty Hours devotions in their little chapel.

> '. . . and their faith and fervour were equal to the occasion. Thanks to the exquisite taste and talent of the Rev. Mother Raphael the Chapel was made to look like a little garden plot of Paradise. High Mass was sung at 7.30 and at its close, the Blessed Sacrament was enthroned. At three o'clock there were special devotions for children; during this service suitable hymns were sung by the little ones with touching earnestness and pathos. The singing both during the Mass and at Benediction was well rendered indeed, and many appreciative remarks to the effectiveness and talent of the choir were made by Catholic visitors.
>
> 'Throughout the day, Rottingdean Catholics supplied a worthy guard of honour round the Blessed Sacrament, each family taking at least two or three turns of watching. The beautiful weather added to the grandeur of the Festa, and as early as 11 o'clock the buses began pouring in a constant stream of visitors from the different Catholic parishes of Brighton. Such holy rivalry, such faith and devotion were never witnessed in Rottingdean before. It was a spectacle that could not and did not fail to arouse the benevolent curiosity of our separated brethren, and many of these asked to be allowed to visit the Chapel. No doubt, Our Blessed Lord gave these even a blessing and our Blessed Lady, the Guide of the Wanderer, the Star of the Sea, must have smiled complacently upon these

> her children also. Solemn Benediction at 5pm brought this never to be forgotten day to a close.'

The magazine reported in February that the *Missa de Angelis* had been excellently rendered by the choir, which had only sung that beautiful Mass for the second time on the Feast of the Epiphany.

## Novena for a new chapel

The Catholic population of the village continued to expand and in the spring of 1918 increasingly strenuous efforts were made to find larger premises to be used as a chapel. These endeavours were spiritual as well as temporal, as evidenced by this extract from the April issue of the *Brighton Catholic Magazine:*

> 'Notice had been given that a general Retreat, or week of Spiritual Exercises would begin on March 17th. All were urged to make this Retreat. Next Father Dreves reminded his hearers that he would like everybody to make a fervent Novena to St. Joseph, in preparation for the great Saint's Feast and that they were to pray for two special intentions to their interests, viz., the Spiritual success of the Retreat, and the finding of much-needed larger local premises, suitable for a temporary chapel. Then, not venturing to ask the congregation to make this Novena in public, the time of the Retreat being so closely at hand, Reverend Father mentioned that he would be in the Chapel every evening during the nine days at six o'clock. Perhaps some who were more leisured than others could come and unite with him, in the presence of Our Blessed Lord, in their prayers to the Foster-Father of Jesus. To the priest's great consolation, the little chapel was nearly crowded every evening and thus what was to be a private act of devotion became a public act of earnest and fervent prayer, which will not be without its special blessings. At the devotions the Rosary was recited, together with an appropriate prayer to St Joseph, and a short Benediction Service, with a blessing with the Ciborium, concluding them every evening.'

On the actual Feast of St Joseph, there was a Sung Mass and the chapel was full. Mrs Stenning and her daughters, Margaret and Janet, who had been received into the Catholic Church on the previous evening, made their first Holy Communion during the Mass that day.

There were soon indications that the Novena to St Joseph had been successful. First came news that the nearby Cliff Tea Rooms were to let. The premises were in a good position and consisted mainly of a large bright and clean hall with ample room for eighty to ninety people. It would have even been large enough to receive the Catholic visitors who came to Rottingdean in summer. However, the rent was £25 a year, plus taxes, to which had to be added the cost of furnishing a chapel, altar vestments, linen, chairs, pictures, and other expenses.

Negotiations over the lease of these tearooms went on for several weeks. At the same time the funding of the resident priest's ministry was a cause for concern. The *Brighton Catholic Magazine* appealed indirectly for a larger contribution from the congregation, stating that:

> 'The collections made at the services average ten shillings (50p) weekly. At the present cost of living, this scarcely leaves the priest with a margin of five shillings (25p) a week for incidental expenses.'

In the May 1918 issue, Father Dreves gratefully acknowledged the donations already sent in to him in answer to the previous month's appeal. These came to £3 2s 6d (£3.12½p), besides the welcome gift of an altar from the Reverend Brother Cyril of Queen's Park. The publication of a list of contributors and benefactors was promised, although in the meantime 'much needed further help' would be received with gratitude.

## Arrivals from Brittany

It was at the end of the 1914-18 war that the Catholic presence in Rottingdean was augmented by the arrival of Father Dreves's sister, Mme Jeanne Achard from Brest, France. She and her stepsister, Aimée, had crossed the Channel on an onion-boat at the turn of the century with the original intention of learning English while staying in a convent in London. However, they both subsequently found work in the capital and it was there that Jeanne met and married a compatriot, Lucien Achard. They had one child, a daughter born in 1910, whom they named Marie-Thérèse. She was left fatherless when Lucien, a flying officer, was shot down in 1917. It was then that Mme Achard moved to Rottingdean with her daughter, who subsequently married and became the Mrs Magee whose notes about people in the parish are referred to in this history and given in full in Appendix I.

Mme Achard acted as landlady to at least one member of the clergy, Father Edmund Baste. He had been chaplain to the Empress Eugénie of France and served as her secretary in connection with correspondence with Pope Benedict XV. By the time he came to Rottingdean, which would have been around 1920, he was 'very aged.' He became ill and was sent to St Joseph's, Bournemouth, where he lived until well into his nineties. She also provided accommodation for the celebrated Portuguese cellist, Guilhermina Suggi who, at the age of twelve, was a member of Oporto City Orchestra and subsequently studied at Leipzig under Pablo Casals, whom she married in 1906. After extensive concert tours she came to live in England in 1914. Her last public appearance was in 1949 at the Edinburgh Festival.

Mme Achard and her daughter returned to France and ran a guest house in Dinard until 1935, then they came back to England. In the 1950s Jeanne Achard retired and went back to her beloved native country, where she died in 1979, aged ninety, near her home town of Brest. Marie-Thérèse remained in England and is now living in Coventry.

## New role for a laundry

On 9 May 1918 the tenancy was secured of a large building in Nevill Road formerly known as the Rottingdean Sanitary Laundry. It had been run by two sisters, the Misses White, who lived in a cottage in the High Street. The premises, which were to serve as a temporary place of worship, or Chapel of Ease, attached to St John the Baptist church, Kemp Town, looked like a good-sized YMCA hut but were in a conveniently central position close to the National School and the High Street.

Although the laundry was qualified by the adjective 'Sanitary,' the *Brighton Catholic Magazine* said that 'the state of the place did not admit or carry with it a literal or common interpretation' of that word. Indeed, while the outside needed only a new coat of paint, the inside was 'more like Bethlehem.' Nevertheless, thanks to handy and energetic help from the Xaverian novices, Father Dreves was able to get most of the rubbish cleared away away in a few days.

No sooner was the Cross placed over the building, than some little birds hastened to build their nest under its shadow, evidently a sign of the fulfilment of God's command to 'increase and multiply.' The earnest wish of Rottingdean's eighty or so resident Catholics was finally met when the new temporary chapel was opened on 7 June 1918, the Feast of the Sacred Heart. The first Benediction was given on the new premises at 3pm by the parish priest of St John the Baptist church.

**The black shed-like structure with two skylights is the former laundry in Nevill Road which served as a temporary chapel from June 1918.**

More than 150 persons were present, together with representatives of Brighton's clergy and religious communities. The Very Reverend Brother Cyril, Provincial of the Xaverians, conducted the singing, which, the magazine reported, was rendered with enthusiasm and fervour by the whole congregation. After Benediction, tea was given to the clergy in Miss Rodber Horton's garden at The Elms. Throughout the day the new chapel, gracefully adorned with flowers, was visited by a number of non-Catholics, all of whom were respectful in their attitude, and not a few contributed to the expenses of the day.

A larger chapel meant the possibility of a large congregation, and the truth of this fact was soon rapidly demonstrated, for following the opening day, attendance at every service, both on weekdays and on Sundays, doubled in number. On Sunday 9 June, both visitors and resident Catholics responded faithfully to Father Dreves's appeal for a General Communion Day to ask the blessings of the Sacred Heart on Rottingdean. There were more than eighty communicants at the First Mass, which was something of a record for the village. At 10 o'clock the Mass was sung by the resident priest in a chapel full to overcrowding. The proper of the Mass was rendered by a special choir of Xaverians from Queen's Park, conducted by the indefatigable

Brother Cyril. The Very Reverend Father Bendon, of Golder's Green, preached at both the morning and evening services. There was another impressive service at 6pm. Again the chapel was packed. Father Bendon preached a devotional sermon on the Sacred Heart, which was followed by the blessing of a banner bearing that symbol. After the blessing, a public act of consecration to the holy image was read by Father Dreves. Benediction, a solemn *Te Deum*, and the hymn to the English Martyrs concluded that memorable Sunday. The Feast of the Assumption of Our Blessed Lady was kept with great fervour, with more than seventy Communions being given. So eager were all to fulfil their duties that Father Dreves had to ask those who had assisted at the Sung Mass to leave the chapel and make room for those who were waiting to come in to the second Mass – and had formed an orderly queue. Of the popularity of the new venue with residents and visitors alike there could be no doubt, since the general attendance at Mass and Benedictions during August 1918 averaged 230 and from the opening date until that month that figure had been 170.

Even when, in October, the weather was inclement, people did not stay away:

> 'The great deluge of rain that visited us on Sunday last was the cause of discomfort to many worshippers, and we will have to call in a professional man to see to those dreadful skylights of ours, and what is worse a pretty heavy bill will have to be met. That the torrential rain did not deter the devout faithful attending Benediction at 6pm on Sunday afternoon to the number of seventy speaks for itself.'

Marie-Thérèse Magee noted that the 'tin roof made the hearing of sermons impossible when it rained'. Kathleen Willson's memories of it are even more vivid:

> 'How could I forget the tin chapel, especially when they started up the generator to make electricity. At the back of the chapel I remember they had the most beautiful picture of Our Lady as you went in the door. It was a lovely picture. I think it had stars around it, big ones, which formed an arch over her head. It was a plain old church, nothing exciting about it. Father Staunton was there'.

Father Lynch-Staunton took over from Father Dreves as priest-in-charge and was here for most of the Twenties. He is still remembered by Nonie Campbell, née Sandever, as he lodged with the family at Field Cottage. She recalls going to Confession accompanied by her mother. All was quiet in the chapel save for the gentle sound of snoring from the box where the priest sat waiting for the next sinner. He was brought back to earth, politely but firmly, by Mrs Sandever.

The chapel was provided relatively quickly with all it needed. On 2 July, the Feast of the Visitation, it was endowed with a statue of Our Lady, Star of the Sea. It was reportedly a very good one, on which the features of the Madonna and Child were exquisitely reproduced, and it added much to the devotional tone of the chapel. Following that acquisition, a statue of the Sacred Heart was sought for the opposite side of the Sanctuary. In August one generous benefactor gave an oak altar and also the Stations of the Cross and in the same month a new white cape was received from the Sisters of Mercy, Bristol Road, Brighton.

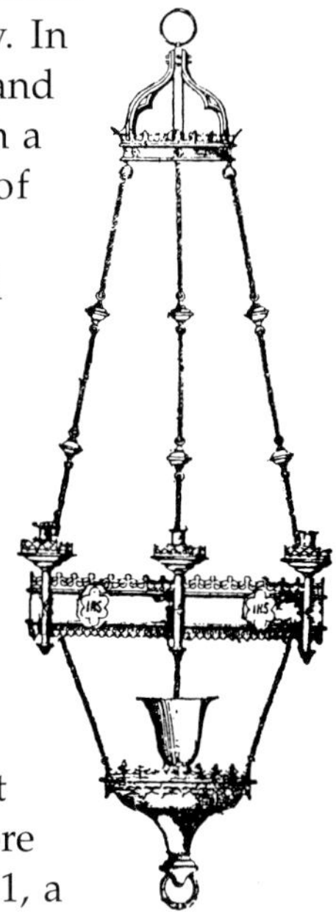

The Sodality of the Children of Mary also worked hard for the new chapel and, under the direction of Mother Henry of the Sacred Heart Convent, made three new sets of vestments for it. Two fine benches with kneelers were also received and, from the same generous benefactor, a church-door case for Catholic Truth Society pamphlets. More than a hundred of these useful publications were soon taken and paid for.

A set of brass candlesticks was acquired with money raised at an impromptu garden fête held at Downlands, then the home of the Pensotti family. More than 100 people attended the event, which raised £21, a substantial sum in those days. In October the blessing of the Stations of the Cross took place and a beautiful Sanctuary lamp was provided by yet another generous donor.

Funds were also needed for the running expenses of the new chapel and more than £21 was raised for this purpose at a concert organised by Miss Marjorie Anderson and 'some kind ladies' under the patronage of the Duchess of Norfolk at the Atheneum Hall, North Street, Brighton. It had originally been planned for 28 November 1918 but had to be postponed to the following January because both organisers and artists were affected by the Spanish 'flu epidemic.

A handwritten document from 1918 entitled *Catholic Church – Rottingdean* has survived. It noted that the temporary chapel was being leased for twelve months and was paying its way. No debts were being incurred. The point was made that at three services held on 18 August, attendance totalled 240, considerably more than the figure for the parish church of St Margaret. During the winter months, by contrast, the worshippers numbered eighty or perhaps 100. It was noted, too, that there were currently ten girls living in Rottingdean who were attending the college at Roedean and who were not allowed to go to Brighton for Mass or Holy Communion. The document ends with this comment about the priest-in-charge:

> 'a Foreigner and very delicate, quite unable to take charge of an ordinary mission.'

## The Father from France

The life the Breton Father Dreves – another of the English Catholic Church's gains from France – was full and productive. Although for much of his priesthood he suffered from ill-health, he lived to be eighty eight and produced his last book at the age of seventy six.

**Father Dreves**

François-Marie Dreves (anglicised form of Drévès) was born in Brest in the diocese of Quimper on 7 June 1887 and later became a naturalised British subject. In his collection of stories, gathered together under the title *A Joyful Herald of the King of Kings*, there are two thinly-veiled autobiographical chapters. These have helped to show his thoughts and development during his formative years. His mother died when he was only four and a much-loved godmother several years later and this cast a shadow over his childhood. His vocation came to him as a boy at a wayside Calvary and for four years he studied with the Benedictines, first in Brest and then for two years in South Wales. In 1907, at the age of twenty, he joined St Peter's College, Freshfield, near Formby on the outskirts of Liverpool. He was happy at the college but after four years of diligence and dedication, he turned his back on his vocation during the holidays, giving himself over to worldly pleasures. The turning point came when he nearly drowned at the seaside. In the delirium after his rescue, he had what is now termed a 'near-death experience', alternately glorious and tormented, and realised the path he should take.

He was happy at college but dogged by ill-health. It was when extremely ill that he was made a member of St Joseph's Society and another episode was so serious that he requested that his ordination, which would normally have taken place in July with missionary work starting in October, be brought forward. His superiors granted the request and the ceremony took place privately in the college chapel on 23 December 1916. He said his first Mass the next day – Christmas Eve. From Freshfield he went to the Dutch college of St Joseph's Missionaries at Roosendaal and then to St Joseph's College, Mill Hill, North London. He was in Rottingdean in 1918, but there is no reference to his stay here in his writings.

In 1926 he was appointed to the Mission of the Upper Nile of Uganda as secretary to Bishop Campling. There his pastoral work, recounted in his book, *The African Chronicle of Brother Giles*, sometimes entailed visits to outlying districts on the back of his lordship's motorbike. When he came home from Uganda in about 1928 he was appointed to a Father Robinson, who had also been in Uganda, to appeal for the missions in the southern dioceses of Southwark and Portsmouth. By 1930 he was in a parish in Northampton, which was followed by Beccles, Oxborough in Norfolk and Wisbech. In the early Thirties he went to Princes Risborough and that became a full-time job for him.

Father Dreves' work in developing the parish of Princes Risborough was a major achievement. When he first went there there was nothing but a temporary old church. The story goes that £3, 000 was needed for a new building. One night two men, wishing to remain anonymous, asked to see him and simply handed him the money. He then acquired a plot on the Aylesbury Road and built his church, which he dedicated to St Theresa and the Child Jesus. It became known as the 'Pilgrim' or 'Wayside' Church and attracted a great following. The foundation stone was blessed by Bishop Youens (himself of French origin) on 28 May 1937. It was consecrated by Bishop Parker of Northampton Diocese in October 1945. Father Dreves had a new presbytery built at Risborough and there he remained until 1950.

From that year until 1965, he was at Courtfield, near Ross-on-Wye, serving as the first rector at this former home of the Vaughan family, whose history he wrote under the title *Remembered in Blessing – The Courtfield Story* (1955).

At Courtfield he established a shrine to Our Lady of Vocations, created a prayer centre for pilgrims; and founded a fervent community of novices training, under experienced guides, to be future missionary brothers. To serve this aim, a new novitiate house was constructed. He also made Courtfield self-supporting by using part of the estate for livestock and arable crops and he refurbished Our Lady's church, adding two side altars.

Father Dreves carried on working right up until 1965, when *With the Help of Our Lady* was published. 'Does old age really matter, especially to a priest if he is told there is still more work he can do?' he wrote on the first page. That same year, he moved to Herbert House, Liverpool, the society's retirement home, where he died peacefully on 23 February 1975 after an active, and in many ways unusual, life.

## The way ahead

With the burgeoning Catholic population in the village, there was increasing pressure for a new centre of worship and education. The good Sisters of St Martha were there to meet these needs for a second time with a new convent and school that would serve Rottingdean for many decades to come.

☆☆☆

# 4

# A time of growth

A HAYFIELD at the north end of the High Street was the site selected for a new Convent of St Martha. It was well away from the winds and spray that beat against its predecessor in winter at the seaward end of the village and was known as The Butt, or 'Rudyard Kipling's Field'. On it the writer had built a small drill hall with an indoor firing range to serve as the headquarters of the Rifle Club he had founded in 1901 in the firm belief that the young men of the village should become familiar with handling rifles in case of war. Kipling was the chairman of the club's committee and he issued precise instructions about the use of the hall during his absences abroad. Meetings and concerts were held there as well as drill, exercises and rifle practice. Smoking was permitted but the drinking of alcohol was forbidden.

The field and its hall were bought by William Hilder, the village butcher, in 1922 and he sold the property to Mother Marguerite Marie two years later. Adjoining the site to the south was Downlands, for many years the home of the Pensotti family. In 1931 it was bought by the convent and renamed Pax. On the northern boundary was Dale Cottage and next to it the house belonging to Sir Roderick Jones, the head of Reuters, and Lady Jones, the novelist and playwright Enid Bagnold. It had formerly belonged to the artist, Sir Edward Burne-Jones, and his wife.

The nuns decided to use a local firm to build their new convent and instructed Messrs Margetts and Cooke to draw up plans based on the design of the mother house in France.

The Margetts and Cooke partnership had been formed in the early 1900s and had acquired the stock and assets of a bankrupt local builder. John Margetts died in 1913 and Arthur S 'Joe' Cooke, whose first job at

**The laying of the foundation stone in the presence of Dr Amigo, Bishop of Southwark and, below, the new Convent of St Martha viewed from The Green.**

the age of sixteen in 1894 was working on a pier for Volk's Rottingdean Railway, was joined in the business by his nephew, Arthur Avis. Cooke went to France to see the mother house for himself and he incorporated many of its architectural features in his design for the new convent, which his firm completed in twelve months. The foundation stone was laid by Mother Marguerite Marie on 21 May 1924 in the presence of Dr Peter Amigo, Bishop of Southwark, and blessed by Father Newton.

A year later a chapel was built behind the convent and became a spiritual focus not only for the sisters but also for Catholics from miles around as a place where Mass could be heard.

At the hectic time of transition between the old Star of the Sea and the new building in the High Street, two children from Dartford were guests of the sisters. Sidney Pile, aged eighty two at the time of writing, and his sister, Alice, had been packed off by their parents, who were in business, for a brief holiday in Rottingdean.

'We commuted between the Star of the Sea, where we ate, and the newly-erected convent, where we slept,' said Sidney when he made a surprise visit to the sisters in 1995.

'One day Alice and I went to the beach and came back with a bucket full of crabs which we put in a corner of a room at the Star of the Sea. When we came back to have a look at them we found the bucket was empty'. The consternation among the sisters that day can be imagined.

## Who was St Martha?

What do we know of the saint after whom the new convent was named other than that she was the sister of Mary and Lazarus, whom Jesus raised from the dead; that she is looked on as the patron of housekeepers and lay sisters; and that she is celebrated on 29 July?

Martha's story is clearly told in the gospels of Luke and John. Both give accounts of the visits Jesus made to Martha's home in Bethany, a small village two miles from Jerusalem.

Luke x, 38-42, tells how Jesus, after delivering the parable of the Good Samaritan:

> . . . came to a village and a woman called Martha welcomed him into her house.
> She had a sister called Mary, who sat down at the Lord's feet and listened to him speaking.

> Now Martha who was distracted with all the serving said, 'Lord, do you not care that my sister is leaving me to do the serving all by myself? Please tell her to help me.' But the Lord answered: 'Martha, Martha,' he said 'you worry and fret about so many things yet few are needed, indeed only one. It is Mary who has chosen the better part; it is not to be taken away from her'.

The next visit, recounted in John xi, 19-45, shows how well Martha learned this lesson. She is grieving the death of her brother Lazarus and her house is full of mourners when she hears that Jesus is coming and goes out to meet him.

> Mary remained sitting in the house. Martha said to Jesus, 'If you had been here, my brother would not have died, but I know that, even now, whatever you will ask of God he will grant you'.
> 'Your brother' said Jesus to her 'will rise again'. Martha said, 'I know he will rise again at the resurrection on the last day'.
> Jesus said: 'I am the resurrection.If anyone believes in me, even though he dies he will live, and whoever lives and believes in me will never die. Do you believe this?'
> 'Yes, Lord,' she said.'I believe that you are the Christ, the Son of God, the one who was to come into this world'.

Martha's conversation with Jesus on this occasion shows her faith and courage. She states clearly without doubt that she believes in Jesus's power, in the resurrection, and most of all that Jesus is the Son of God. Jesus tells her that he is the resurrection and the life and then goes on to raise her brother from the dead.

The final picture of Martha in the gospels is in John xii, 2-3 when, six days before the Passover, Jesus was in Bethany again:

> . . . where Lazarus was, whom he had raised from the dead. They gave a dinner for him there; Martha waited on them and Lazarus was among those at table.
> Mary brought in a pound of very costly ointment, pure nard, and with it anointed the feet of Jesus, wiping them with her hair; the house was full of the scent of the ointment'.

Once again Martha is not in the spotlight, she is not the subject of a impressive miracles, she does not cause a commotion at dinner by anointing Jesus with expensive perfume. Martha simply served Jesus.

In a text entitled, *Monuments inédits de l'Apostolat de Sainte Madeleine,* Martha is credited with performing a miracle herself. It relates that, after the crucifixion, many of the disciples gathered at her home, which they unanimously decided to convert into a basilica. At the gathering, the number of guests was large and the wine supply was soon exhausted. Martha, never neglectful of her duties as a hostess, knelt in silent prayer and miraculously transformed the water in the pots into wine, in precise imitation of the miracle performed by Jesus at the marriage feast of Cana.

There are no further scriptural references to Martha or what became of her. However, a totally untrustworthy legend says that during the persecution which followed the early teaching of the Apostles, the Jews turned in anger on Martha's family. They put her on board a ship with Mary and Lazarus, Marcella a maid, and someone named Maximin and cast all five adrift without food and with no means of steering, so that they should meet their deaths. However, guided by Divine Providence, the craft arrived safely at a place near Marseilles where, after converting its people, Lazarus became the first bishop and Maximin the first Bishop of Aix. Martha and Mary lived in retirement.

According to another legend a fearful monster lived near Marseilles and its very breath caused the death of those it approached. One day, so the story goes, Martha went out alone to encounter the dragon and, slipping a cord round its neck, forced it to follow her, much to the amazement of the inhabitants. Then, in some unrecorded way, she put the creature to death and so became the object of the people's veneration.

## The garden statue of St Martha

When he unveiled a statue of St Martha in the convent garden on 20 May 1928, the Reverend G Nicholson aptly alluded to the legends concerning the saint.

He said that in much the same way as Martha and her companions had arrived near Marseilles, the Sisters of St Martha had arrived in southern England twenty five years earlier and out of their poverty had provided a beautiful little chapel. Its importance for the needs of the district was well known to all. He wondered what the Protestants in the village sometimes thought about the sisters. Several institutions, convents among them, were a source of deep mystery to the public mind. 'What,' people asked, 'do the sisters do all day long?' Unable to appreciate the beauty of a life devoted to God, they made many curious surmises in answer to the question. He believed the new statue would prompt many inquiries among passers-by as to the work of the sisters and their religion. They would come to the convent door, perhaps to seek enlightment or recieve instruction.

Pointing to the statue of St Martha, Father Nicholson went on to suggest that there might be some who would ask why a dragon was represented with her. In his view, the dragon had a wider meaning:

> 'It is symbolic of heresy. Many in England are the victims of its poisonous breath. St Martha has come to this very Protestant corner of England to combat it. Overlooking the village, Martha faces the ancient village church built centuries ago by Catholic hands. There, Catholics once gathered to hear Mass; there they sought pardon for their sins and there they knelt to receive Holy Communion. I pray that the day might come when England will embrace once again the old religion and the village church of Rottingdean will be Catholic again'.

It is more than seventy years since this address was made in the presence of Mother Bénédicte, the Assistant-General from Le Bugue, representing Mother St Pierre, the Superior-General, who was unable to attend the ceremony.

People and churches have changed. Ecumenism has come a long way. In this third millennium, the two churches in the village and in the neighbouring parishes are perhaps closer in thought and action than they have ever been. As for the work and the outlook of the Sisters of St Martha, the characteristics that have stayed with them down the years have been a deep faith, a certain family spirit, a happy lack of pointless restrictions, a ready welcome for all and a spirit of cheerful giving. These are the characteristics that have made possible a life of service to Our Lord and concern for the least of his brethren.

## The convent chapel

In Rottingdean, 'neath the Sussex Downs
Where drowsy sheep oft graze,
And soft sea breezes ever blow,
To cool the hottest days.
Guarded by a statue white,
Lies the Convent that I love,
'Tis here that restful blessed peace,
Is showered by God above.

The Convent Chapel is quite famed,
Tho' it is small and neat,
Our Lady Star of the Sea 'tis named.
And here the children's voices sweet,
Are often heard at even-tide,
As to God above they softly rise.
Sure ! there's no lovelier place I'll find,
Till I'm above the skies

These lines were written by a twelve year old pupil at the convent, Jeanne Lawrence. The chapel which inspired such affection had been completed when she was an infant and was to serve the needs of Catholics from miles around for more than thirty years until the Church of Our Lady of Lourdes was built. Today Mass is still said there a few times each week.

It was not until the chapel had been in use for some five years that it was decorated with the magnificent stained glass it has today. In the semi-circle behind the altar is a triptych depicting three archangels – as there is in St Margaret's church across The Green. There the triptych is by Sir Edward Burne-Jones and was installed in 1893, the year this painter of the Pre-Raphaelite school and pupil of Rossetti resigned his Associateship of the Royal Academy.

The artist responsible for the chapel window is not known but the style is reminiscent of the imaginary medievalism of the Pre-Raphaelites. The window on the left depicts the Archangel Raphael, the travelling companion of Tobit's son, Tobias, who is shown as a young man holding a fish. This is an allusion to an incident described in the Book of Tobit vi, 2-9 in which the angel instructs the youth in

**The archangels' triptych behind the altar in the convent chapel.**

the healing qualities of the heart, gall and liver of a fish – 'for these have curative properties.' At the foot of the window are the initials FP and a reference to Tobit xii, 7 'It is right to keep the secrets of a king; yet right to reveal and publish the works of God. Thank him worthily. Do what is good, and no evil can befall you.'

The archangel Michael, in his Revelations' xii, 7-9 role as 'captain of the heavenly host' occupies the centre window. He is in full armour, carries a banner with the words *Quis ut dei* – 'Who is like God? – and is in process of overcoming evil in the form of a green dragon. This window has the initials FB and the date 1921. The reference is to 2 Timothy iv, 7 'I have fought the good fight to the end; I have run the race to the finish; I have kept the faith.'

The right-hand window has Gabriel, the angel of the Annunciation, telling the Virgin Mary that she will conceive and give birth to Jesus. Below are the words 'Re DeV' and the text is Luke i, 37 'For nothing is impossible to God.' On the left wall as one faces the altar is a window depicting St Anne, the mother of Mary, teaching her daughter to read. The window, dated 1931, commemorates one Annie Burke.

Behind the gallery is a window to Margaret Mary O'Connor endowed in October 1932. It shows a nun kneeling before Jesus with the light from his Sacred Heart shining upon her. She is St Margaret Mary Alacoque who, between 1673 and 1675, had four visions of Christ concerning devotions to his heart as symbolizing his love for mankind, and was charged to promote this devotion. Below is the Latin inscription from Proverbs xxxi, 31 'Give her a share in what her hands have worked for, and let her works tell her praises as the city gates' and the words 'Pray for M M O'Connor'.

Returning to the left-hand wall as one faces the altar there is a plaque in memory of nine year old Peter Funnell who died of meningitis in March 1934. Peter and his brother Geoffrey, four years his junior, of Park Road, Rottingdean, were the sons of Police Constable Edmund Funnell, whose father and grandfather had both been kennel huntsmen with the celebrated Brookside Harriers.

**Peter Funnell, whose happy childhood was cut short.**

## Maurice Baring – and friends

The chapel welcomed a number of prominent worshippers during the first decade its doors were open to the villagers. Among the most notable was Maurice Baring, novelist, dramatist, poet and critic, fifth son of the banker, Baron Revelstoke. One of the stained glass windows testifies to his generosity and faith. It is dated 1931 and depicts St George beneath which is inscribed *Propositi tenax* – 'Firm of purpose'. He had moved to Rottingdean in 1928 and joined the faithful for Mass at the convent, even though he had a private chapel at his home – Half Way House in Steyning Road where the Highbury House Rest Home now stands.

Baring was, on occasion, accompanied to the convent chapel by Hilaire Belloc and Gilbert Keith Chesterton. These literary giants were not always recognised by the sisters, as happened in an instance described in a talk by Mrs Collette Flanagan, headmistress of Rottingdean's RC Primary School from 1969 to 1981:

> 'One day, after Holy Mass, Maurice and Hilaire went off, leaving Gilbert at his prayers. Mother Christine, who was French, went into the chapel and saw him there alone. She looked suspiciously at this great bulk of a man, who looked, in her eyes, like a tramp. She was very uneasy about him, and eventually left the chapel to seek help. She came across Sister St Aubyn "Oh Sister, will you please do something – a man looking very much like a tramp is in the chapel and I am very worried about it". Sister St Aubyn went to investigate and she, of course, at once recognised the great man himself.'

Baring was something of an eccentric and a notorious practical joker. He was also an outstanding linguist, eventually mastering numerous languages, yet despite being born into a distinguished banking family he was barely numerate.

**Maurice Baring absorbed in a game of patience in Half Way House.**

He was educated at Eton and Trinity College, Cambridge. He joined the Diplomatic Service in 1898 and was posted to Paris, Rome and Copenhagen. In 1904 he left the Service and took up journalism, going initially to Russia as the correspondent of the *Morning Post*. In 1912 he moved to *The Times*, and became its special correspondent in the Balkans. During the First World War, Baring served with distinction as a staff officer in the Royal Flying Corps. After the war, he turned to the novel and his first venture in that field, *Passing By*, was published in 1921. The subtle and charming portraits of his own milieu which followed, among them *C*,

*Cat's Cradle* and *Daphne Adeane*, are not, however, much read today. He wrote forty three books between 1902 and 1936, covering the fields of travel, literary criticism, autobiography, verse, plays and novels. In all he published some eighty volumes.

Baring came from a Protestant family – indeed, his father built a church near their West Country retreat. At Cambridge, which he left without taking a degree, he faced the reaction against Christianity which seems to characterise younger intellectual élites. He was told by one member of such a group that he 'ought not to go to chapel, as it was setting a bad example. Christianity was exploded, a thing of the past'. In the winter of 1893, on his return from Berlin, he was asked why he did not go to church, to which he replied that he did not believe in a Christian faith. If he were ever to again, he added, he would be a Catholic.

During his gradual conversion, which spanned ten years, Baring was in constant touch with Hilaire Belloc, asking for information and exchanging views and opinions. Their first meeting had hardly been auspicious as Belloc had told him that he (Baring) would most certainly go to hell. However, on their second meeting in Oxford, where Hilary, as Baring called him, lived in a charming little house in Holywell and was coaching young pupils, they did indeed become friends.

On a visit to Rome in February 1902, he was profoundly impressed by the ritual and the magnificence of the Church when Pope Leo XIII celebrated his jubilee. He heard him officiate at Mass at the Sistine Chapel and also went to High Mass at St Peter's when the Pope was carried in on his chair and blessed the crowd.

Baring, who was finally received into the Catholic church at Brompton Oratory in 1909, became a close friend of Enid Bagnold of *National Velvet* fame. In her autobiography, she describes their first meeting:

> 'When Maurice Baring came to live in Rottingdean. . . Desmond [MacCarthy] had the impudence to say he wouldn't like me. But there was mischief in his voice. Maurice asked me to dine with him alone. It was a nightmare. He was so alarmingly shy himself that he made me as tongue-tied. If I said anything 'clever' he instantly asked his butler to bring some bread. I couldn't repeat it: I couldn't go again. I didn't'.

A year or two later, Baring's great friend Laura Lovat came to see her, saying that Maurice wanted her to go and see him. By this time he was very ill with paralysis agitans. Reluctantly, Enid Bagnold went that evening at six:

> 'I found him in his back garden, in a wheel-chair, his hard straw hat crammed on his red face. He had been feeding the birds in the garden. We opened on that. It didn't go very far and we were back on jerks of talk, irrelevant subjects caught up in desperation. At half past six (which was all I could manage) I got up, mumbling goodnight to the children. He didn't detain me but looked up from his chair with his curious smile.
> 'Come again.'
> 'When?'
> 'Tomorrow night. Same time.'

She went, virtually every night for years. When she was unable to, she would send one of her children, usually Dominic, her youngest, or Laurian, then in her teens. She found it an ordeal, mainly because of the long silences. She had never known him in his 'larky brilliant days.'

Ill as he was, she felt he needed the company of a pet and finally decided on a budgerigar, to be named Dempsey. As a present he was given a counterpane, made by the Jones family, including Roderick, when ski-ing in Switzerland. It was embroidered in black thread on white linen squares on which were the names of his forty three books. Round the margin young Laurian Jones had worked a border of galloping horses in black. It is still in her possession at her home in France, hanging at the entrance to the guest bedroom, having been passed to her by one of Baring's nieces or great-nieces.

**The private chapel in Half Way House.**

By 1940 the stress and dangers of the war, combined with his dreadful affliction, forced him to move away and stay with Lord and Lady Lovat at Beaufort Castle in distant Inverness. He never returned to Rottingdean. When he was told that the bomb which fell on Half Way House in December 1942 had entirely obliterated the chapel as well as half the house, his one regret was that the chapel had suffered most. But he never referred to this great loss again. Maurice Baring was released from his suffering on 14 December 1945 and was buried in a remote valley in the shadow of a highland church near a river lined with silver birches. A timeless haven, where his spirit is free.

## Alfred Noyes

Another local literary figure, although not a Catholic, was the poet Alfred Noyes who spent fifteen years in Rottingdean in the early 1900s. He, like Baring, lived in Steyning Road, in a house named Ewhurst, now the Braemar Guest House. Jim Copper, Bob's father, remembered him as:

> '. . . a most imposing figure, dressed in a long, dark cloak and black, wide-brimmed felt hat. He could often be seen striding along over the downs at the back of the village or seated on the corner of Vicarage Laine on top of a steep bank above a chalk road. From this vantage point he could look right over the village in the valley across to the black windmill on the opposite hill and down southwards out to sea.'

Here in Rottingdean Noyes produced some of his memorable poems, including *The Silver Crook, The Sussex Sailor*, *The Tramp Transfigured* and *Tales of the Mermaid Tavern.*

## A link with the past is broken

On 3 March 1932 a major link with the past was broken with the death of the Reverend Mother, Marguerite Marie Lajoumard, the foundress of the Sisters of St Martha in England and first Superior of the convent in Rottingdean.

She was initially buried in the churchyard of St Margaret's but on 14 August 1936 the grave was re-opened and the body was re-interred in the tiny cemetery of St Martha's Convent. She lies a few yards behind the statue of St Martha on high ground overlooking the village and sea.

## Jillisen stays on

Jillisen Taylor, who attended the Star of the Sea convent during the four years her parents were at Manor Cottage, insisted, when the family returned to Rottingdean from Newmarket for the second and last time, on going to St Martha's convent. The Taylors stayed briefly in Brighton before renting West House but Jillisen refused to attend the private schools her sisters went to.

The year was 1928 and she was twelve years old. Her time at the convent would be relatively short as the sisters were then only taking pupils up to the age of fourteen and did not offer the School Certificate. Jillisen determined to stay on an extra year. Looking back, she realises that this was wilfulness on her part – 'it really was a wasted year', she said – but she treasures the memory of that extended stay in so peaceful and warm an environment. She had private lessons and in other classes, such as French, followed the younger ones. She well remembers:

> 'dear Father Keogh, with his white hair, yet he was not all that old. He was very nice. He used to come once a week, I think on Tuesdays.'

It was during one of his catechism lessons that the light of Catholicism entered her life:

> 'I was given permission to sit in on the class. I thought ''These children, they know God, they know something about him and I know nothing. What they've got, I want.'' I can remember the actual moment . . . it was strange. I was sitting at the back and I remember the girl, this lovely girl, who answered Father's question ''What are the four marks of the Church?'' The answer was: ''One, holy, Catholic and apostolic.'' I suddenly saw the light.'

She said nothing to anyone, however, as she was leaving at the end of that term. She went to Lourdes Convent in Brighton and waited until she was twenty one before becoming a nun. She felt her parents would never have given their consent, yet they respected her decision when the time came.

Sister Veronica had taken Jillisen and two other pupils for a short holiday at the Mother House in Périgueux before the war. When Jillisen went back to France to serve as a postulant, war had broken out and, like so many others, she was cut off completely from England.

'The propaganda was terrible', she said. 'If I'd believed it, Brighton didn't exist any more. I was in the mother house in Nevers, which was

**Pax, formerly Downlands, the house for the boarders in the High street, was later linked to the convent by a covered passage.**

then at Brive, near Bordeaux. I loved the Sisters of St Martha but you can't choose your Order because the Lord knows where he wants you to go. The sisters at Rottingdean were so good. They understood. I loved them and still go back to see them although I haven't been lately'.

A fellow pupil and great friend, Betty Hewetson, 1915-1979, also became a nun and did join the Order of St Martha, as Sister Margaret Mary, taking her name from Rottingdean's Reverend Mother. She made her profession early in the war and spent many years in Rottingdean, where she taught music and singing. In later life she transferred to the convent at High Barnet. Although she died there, her wish to be buried in Rottingdean was fulfilled.

Jillisen made profession under the name Marie-Christine – the 'Marie' being added later to the 'Christine' which was taken from the name of the Assistant at Rottingdean.

☆ ☆ ☆

**The children had their own garden at the convent, and this postcard from the Thirties shows them tending it diligently.**

**One of the classrooms of the convent.**

# 5

# Convent schooldays

WHEN the Sisters of St Martha's Convent bought the neighbouring property, Downlands, they renamed it Pax and used it to expand the school, which then had thirty pupils, to take in boarders.

A school magazine entitled *St Martha's Convent, Rottingdean,* was first published in October 1935. It was dedicated to 'the Respectful and Loving Memory of our dearly regretted REV MOTHER MARGARET' and written and put together by pupils of different ages. The contents show what the youngsters themselves thought of the developments within and outside the classroom.

September 19 saw the pupils return to school to find that the middle classroom had been newly decorated in cream and brown and that the kindergarten had been transferred to Pax.

In an article on the chapel contributed by 'An Admirer' was the comment that the building was 'alas! much too small for the ever increasing flow of visitors to the little village on the Sussex Coast', and an appeal was made for legacies.

On 20-26 January 1936, the school followed the death, lying-in-state and funeral of King George V. Some of the girls went to London for the occasion. Twice there was Exposition of the Blessed Sacrament in the chapel when prayers were said for the repose of the king's soul, for the future welfare of the Empire and for the new king, Edward VIII.

Some weeks earlier had come the news of the death of Princess Victoria, who had visited the convent twice a few years earlier during her stay in Rottingdean. On the return to school after the half-term holiday the pupils welcomed four newcomers, all sisters: Cecilia, Joan, Helen and Anne Cooke.

In March, Denise and Patsy Andre, pupils of Miss Hewetson, opened a season of musical successes by gaining certificates for pianoforte at the London Music Festival. Later that month three pupils went in for a LAMDA elocution exam in Brighton and passed 'very brilliantly.' At the Brighton Music Festival in May, some of the girls carried off high marks for piano playing.

Walks and excursions were often arranged. Early in the Easter term a ten mile walk was accomplished 'without any serious fatigue'. Another walk took the pupils to St John the Baptist at Kemp Town and back, with no 'serious detriment to our legs but an enormous increase in our appetites'.

Telscombe village was visited on a sunny afternoon in June, when the girls donned their cotton frocks for the first time. Bathing excursions occasionally took place, too, as on the Feast of Saints Peter and Paul when the pupils returned in the evening to do justice to a high-class tea. In July, Form IV set off in glorious sunshine for the joys of Arundel, visiting the castle, boating on the river, roaming through the woods and enjoying a coach drive along the coast road.

Sundays in May were celebrated by processions through the convent grounds and on Rogation Days there were processions at 7.15am accompanied by the singing of the Litany of the Saints. On the feast of Corpus Christi there was also a procession round the grounds.

At an Exhibition and Sale of Needlework 'all vied with each other in the selling of sweets, shilling teas and goods of all kinds' reports the magazine. Joan Linnell, aged fifteen, described the event in detail:

> 'The stalls were varied and tastefully arranged, displaying to the best advantage the various works of art of the pupils of St Martha's – embroidered fancy articles suitable to all tastes; babies' frocks, boots, bonnets all in wool, pinafores of every description, and last but not the least a stall containing nick-nacks (all hand made) which soon disappeared at 6d each. The drawings too, attracted a good many spectators and all were universal in their praise of the artistic talent of some of our seniors.
>
> 'Out on the well-kept lawns, chairs and tables with gaily-coloured cloths were arranged at which sat groups of happy people, enjoying tasty sandwiches and delicious home-made cakes. Beneath the trees on the far side was a stall which proudly displayed its burden of home-made cakes and sweets. . . Some of the girls, the stall-holders, were in fancy dress, while others wore their gayest summer frocks, which added to the charm

**A garden party in progress 'out on the well kept lawns . . .'**

> and colour of this joyous afternoon. At five o'clock, another surprise was awaiting the visitors for different songs and dances were performed by the pupils, to the great delight of all present. French Elocution was eagerly listened to, and received with, unanimous praise and appreciation.'

On a more sombre note, the pupils were sad to read, on 4 July, the news of the death of G K Chesterton the previous month:

> '. . . we agree with the whole Catholic population that the Church in England has lost a friend and English Catholic literature one of its best supporters. We shall never more have the pleasure of seeing this fatherly figure in our little chapel, but we pray that God may reward him for his life of devotedness and self-sacrifice in the interests of Catholic action.'

## The summer term of 1937

An almost daily diary of events was published in the school magazine in the autumn under the title *Summer Term Review 1937.* This was the last summer of real peace. Ahead was the Munich crisis and, after the harvest of 1939, came the war that changed the world. The review encapsulates the interests and activities of a group of, admittedly privileged youngsters, living and learning in a religious rather than secular context. Here it is, just as it appeared in the magazine:

> 19th April. We returned to school very excited and looking forward to the joys, and thrills of the summer term. On arriving we found Reverend Mother General at the convent. She came to visit us and she spoke to us in French and congratulated us on our knowledge of that language.
> 29th April. Monica, one of our boarders, left with Sister for Lourdes. We all envied her and wished we had the happiness of going too.
> 6th May. We had a holiday as it was Ascension Day, and enjoyed a breezy walk.
> 11th May. We were allowed home for a week in honour of the Coronation. Some of us were lucky enough to visit London and were happy spectators of the never-to-be-forgotten scene.
> 19th May. We returned to school and set to work with extra zeal for the fast-approaching examinations.
> 24th May. Two of our pupils went to Brighton to take part in the Music Festival, both did very well, one receiving a certificate.
> 25th May. Four other pupils entered for the Festival, all played very well.
> 30 May. A beautiful day of glorious sunshine. We had our Corpus Christi Procession in the grounds. Everything was very beautiful, including the singing, and the children all in white.
> 1st June. Catechism Examination. All did very well. The lucky winner of the medal was Diana Byles. Eighteen others received certificates.
> 6th June. Another day of beautiful sunshine for the Newhaven Procession. Thirty-five of us, all in white, went to this procession, we were only one of the many schools present.
> 7th June. The report of our Catechism examination arrived, we are pleased to say it was 'Excellent'.
> 9th June. Our first day in swimming.
> 14th June. Our Examinations began. Oh! what a week of labour! We all meant to do our very best.
> 29th June. A holiday for the feast of Saint Peter and Saint Paul. We went for walks and played tennis.
> 3rd July. The long-waited-for day on which we held our annual sale of work, needlework exhibition, and concert. All three were great successes from every point of view.

5th July. Mr. Septimus Pears gave us a lantern lecture in the gym. The subject chosen was 'The Tower of London', we all enjoyed it immensely and found it very instructive and interesting.
8th July. We had our annual Sports Day, and were favoured with glorious sunshine and mild sea-breezes.
14th July. We took the train to Bramber Castle for our summer outing. It was a lovely sunny day. We had a wonderful time and thoroughly enjoyed every minute of it.

## The first wedding

The convent had received a Certificate of Registry for the solemnisation of matrimony on 5 July 1937 and the first wedding took place there a fortnight later. The bride was a former pupil of St. Martha's, Isabelle Sandever, and the bridegroom was a former jockey, Bernard McHardy, the model for Mi Taylor in *National Velvet.* It was a memorable day for the pupils as well as for the principal participants and the *Summer Term Review* carried this enchanting account of the proceedings.

The 19th July was eagerly anticipated by young and old in Rottingdean, but none looked forward to that day with such keen interest as did our dear Sisters and ourselves. On that day we were to witness the first wedding in our little Chapel. Any wedding is exciting, but this one was doubly so. Our readers will pardon our enthusiasm when they realize that the first bride to walk up the Chapel path was Miss Isabelle Sandever, an old pupil of St Martha's and a very popular young lady in the village.

In the year 1903, when the Sisters of St Martha first came from France, to found a convent in Rottingdean, the bride's grandmother, Mrs Hennessey, very cordially received them, conducted them to the house they were to occupy, and presented them with the keys. How fitting it was, then, that the granddaughter of this courteous lady should be the first young bride to smile happily from our Chapel steps as she crossed the threshold of a new life.

At 9.30 on the morning of the 19th July, all the wedding guests arrived in good time for the ceremony which was to take place, with Nuptial Mass, at 10 o'clock. Our little Chapel barely accommodated the congregation. The bridegroom, Mr Bernard McHardy, one of the pillars of the chapel and a general favourite, attended by his brother, joined the expectant crowd. It only now needed the presence of the bride to complete the happiness of all gathered together to witness the union. At last she appeared, coming up the Convent path, a vision in white, as she walked along in the glorious July sunshine. None of us are superstitious, yet I'm sure every one of us, as we watched her approach, thought of the adage, "Happy is the bride that the sun shines on." She was clad in a snow-white dress of gleaming satin, the simplicity of the make only enhanced the charm of the wearer, who looked so young and child-like with her clustering curls peeping out from under her wreath and flowing veil. After the bride, came her sister, Miss Nonie Sandever the bridesmaid, charmingly attired in pink.

**'The happy pair'.**

When Miss Sandever reached the altar, which was most beautifully decorated for the occasion, she was given away by her father. We all felt very touched as we looked down on the happy pair plighting their troth at the altar-steps, oblivious of all around them, save Our Divine Lord, His minister and themselves. During the Mass, the Rev Father Hill gave an appropriate little sermon on the seriousness of the step these two young people had taken.

When Mass was ended the radiant bride passed down the Chapel aisle leaning on her husband's arm, while the organ played the lively strains of the Wedding March. . .

In her biography of Enid Bagnold, Anne Sebba describes McHardy as a strong-minded personality who:

'. . . with his slight build, curly red hair and leathered face, looked every inch the former steeplechase jockey he was. But he had given up professional riding by the time he came to Rottingdean unemployed and hoping to find work among the still plentiful racing stables and livery owners of the village. He stayed longer than he might have done because he fell in love with a pretty local girl, Isabelle Sandever. At seventeen, she was ten years his junior. McHardy was a devout Catholic and usually went home every summer to the remote Caldy Island, off the coast of Wales, where his family ran a farm for a group of Benedictine monks. But one summer, to be near Isabelle, he stayed in Sussex and found a job teaching the Asquith children to ride. General Arthur and Mrs Betty Asquith and their four daughters, Mary, Jean, Susan and Christine, had, since 1928, taken a house on Rottingdean Green for the summer months: Kipling's former residence, The Elms, which now belonged to the Joneses. The Asquiths introduced the Joneses to riding as Jean, Sue and Laurian became immediate, close friends'.

McHardy's blend of romance, religion and toughness captivated Enid Bagnold and worked on her imagination. She wanted him both as a teacher for her children and as a character in a story, for there was an air of mystery about McHardy. Enid knew all about the yellowing newspaper cutting showing a horse falling under its rider which McHardy carried around with him. She, believing that he had lost his nerve after a dramatic fall in an important race in Belgium, invented a glorious past for him. But Isabelle maintains his racing career had been a much more humdrum affair with no dramatic falls or loss of nerve.

## A new passage to Pax

The construction work on a new and long-awaited covered passage between the convent and Pax to join up both houses began in May 1937. An army of workmen toiled away in the grounds and the walls of the new structure reportedly rose with 'amazing rapidity'. Each day the pupils eagerly looked for the new rows of bricks, until at last they saw the roof completed. The outside of the passage was in keeping with the old garden walls, and the roof was like that of the convent. Inside it had cream walls, and windows down one side looking onto the gardens and Pax's lawn. On 8 July it was finished, and the workmen were given a high tea on the lawn – a fitting ending to their weeks of strenuous labour. On the day of the opening ceremony, the pupils lined up at the entrance at 10am. Canon Newton cut the velvet knot to allow the procession to pass through, and the new walls of the cloister echoed to joyful voices singing the Litanies of the Saints. The generosity of an unnamed woman benefactor was acknowledged – without it the work could not have been carried out.

Two doubles games in play on the tennis courts.

The statue of Our Lady brought from France by the exiled Sisters of St Martha kept watch over the convent from the garden. It is now in a specially-built grotto on roughly the same site.

## More memories

Jean Rattrie, née Lunnon, was born in 1932 and was one of three sisters who attended the convent. She now lives in New Zealand, where she and her husband, a native of Maryport, Carlisle, are enjoying their retirement from their mixed farming business in South Auckland. She has only happy memories of her convent schooldays:

'When I first went to school at the convent, it was still called Star of the Sea and later became St Martha's. Our brown uniform had a beret for winter wear which had an enamel star pinned to it which could be used as a really lethal weapon if required. Those badges were the bane of my life, expensive and so easily chipped when not treated properly. They were later replaced by cloth badges.

'I think I went to school before I was five, but records may show that my first teacher was Miss Agnes Fleming – one of a kind: tweeds, pork pie hat and in winter, on walks over the downs, always galoshes. Tall and spare, she lived in Pax, the annexe to the convent. She was the infant teacher until she retired and left an indelible impression.The other lay teachers I remember are Miss Kelly, who finally left to marry a soldier, and Miss Payne, who succeeded Miss Fleming as infant teacher and was also art teacher to all the classes.

'Sister St Gerard was headmistress and I loved her dearly, also Sister Veronica, who I think was more on the housekeeping side of running the convent; Sister Lucienne, who taught me how to polish a floor with rag pads tied round both feet which could get into corners and were great for getting up sliding speed in the corridors. It made work fun. After the war, I believe Sister Lucienne returned to France. Sister Avite, small, dumpy and very French, was chief cook and the meals were good. I particularly remember haricot beans.

'The atmosphere was always serene. Mostly the nuns moved around very quietly but one could always hear the rattle of the large rosary beads they wore at their waist. We were well grounded in manners and deportment and were aware, even as very young children, that we were surrounded by really good women. My own conversion to Catholicism was a direct result of their benign supervision. I can say with total conviction that St Martha's, the nuns and lay teachers all contributed to my very happy childhood spent in Rottingdean.

It was in the summer of 1937 that Adèle Aldridge started her five year spell of attendance at St Martha's. She was born in Perth, Western Australia, and had moved with her parents to Saltdean from Ruislip that year at the age of ten. Adèle's memories are also happy ones:

> 'I loved it there, I really did. Both Sister St Gerard and Sister Veronica were exceedingly nice nuns.
> 'No sciences or domestic subjects, other than needlework, were taught, although the sisters had applied, without success, to the authorities for the facilities to offer them. There were two French nuns among their number, Sister Lucienne and Sister Géneviève, but I do not recall either of them actually teaching that language.
> 'A handful of boys were among the pupils.. They were normally taken up to the age of eight, but when the war came this limit was raised.'

Adèle's parents always made the serving parish priest welcome in their home, even though her father was not a Catholic. 'Nick' Aldridge, as he was always known, lived to the grand old age of ninety four and got on famously with Father Vivian St Clare Hill. Both were veterans of the Great War, in which the priest had been gassed, and many an evening was spent exchanging yarns and anecdotes. Father Hill's successor, Father James Austin, lived in a small bungalow in Chailey Avenue, near its junction with Steyning Road and was also a friend of the family. After Rottingdean, he went on to build the church of St John Vianney at Bexley Heath, Kent.

In the last few years of peace, the convent, with its school and chapel, remained the tranquil heart of Catholic education and worship in Rottingdean.

## The village in wartime

In 1938, Colonel Weekes of the British Red Cross Society visited Rottingdean to inspect the Sussex 172 (Rottingdean) Detachment and present chemical warfare and First Aid certificates. It was his opinion that Sussex was hardly a military objective and that it was unlikely Hitler would send bombers here. Later events proved how wrong he was, and bore out the assertion made six years earlier by Prime Minister Stanley Baldwin, a former resident of Rottingdean, that 'the bomber will always get through'.

Elementary precautions were taken against aerial bombardment. The village hall became an ARP post and First Aid centre. Mock exercises were regularly held, with 'casualties' labelled with their injuries. Near West Street a fire station with a complement of seven firemen was established and a number of air-raid shelters were built. An observation

**A policeman was killed and seven people were injured when a Dornier dropped four bombs on the village in December 1942.**

post served by a telephone line was set up high on Beacon Hill while a small gun emplacement was located further over the hill; along the clifftops there were ack-ack guns. There was, reportedly, a wireless monitoring unit in one of the houses at the top of Nevill Road.

Although Rottingdean emerged unscathed from the Luftwaffe's first phase of attacks it was among the coastal targets which suffered tip-and-run raids until 1944.

Mrs Patty Bishop, née Haslitt, of Ovingdean remembers regarding those distant days as 'one great adventure'. She was enrolled at the convent in 1939 at the age of seven, having come from South London.

'As children we discovered all the excitement of war. The planes that droned over every night, the sirens, a few bombs on Rottingdean (one down the lift shaft in the flats near the coast road, two on the Downs) and the nightly trek down to the shelters, all of us in our dressing-gowns with eiderdowns and teddy bears. Our shelters were of a sort of cage type, with thick wire sides, a solid steel top and a mattress where about four of us slept top to tail. Some nights we climbed out of the windows in the long cloakroom where some of the shelters were and our lockers, and would watch the dog fights overhead and over the sea. The poor nuns nearly had a fit, especially when they found the gooseberries, etc. were also missing.'

Like so many towns and villages in the south, Rottingdean was invaded by evacuees from London, who were were labelled-up and allocated among the villagers. When a contingent arrived in September 1939, a clinic was opened in the room above the garage at Norton House opposite the Pond and the new arrivals treated with the help of Dr Webb for a variety of ailments, the most common being impetigo and head lice.

The need to get away from the capital brought an influx of residents to the village during the war years and some settled here permanently. The Whatleys, whose London home had been bombed, rented Lavender Cottage in Dean Court Road, opposite the Tudor Close Hotel, for some months in 1942. Reginald, his wife, Victoria, and their two daughters, Barbara and Diane, then moved to a bungalow in Hailsham Avenue on Saltdean Mount and during the week Reginald continued to serve as an ARP warden in London. Later they bought a house in Stanmer Avenue and here the girls grew up and went to school at St Martha's – Barbara from 1944 and Diane from 1946. Both sisters now look back on the convent and nuns with the fondest affection. Barbara, who launched a successful fund towards the refurbishment of the chapel in 1990, maintained close ties with her beloved convent by staying there for a weekly spring and autumn holiday with her mother until the latter's death in 1997.

On 18 December 1942 one of three Dornier Do 217s that had flown low over the Channel to strafe Brighton dropped its bombs on the sea front. The policeman on point duty at the crossroads, War Reserve Constable Harold Stone, died from the injuries caused by fragments of debris resulting from the explosion. In the basement of St Aubyn's school, used by the Fire Service, Bernard McHardy was knocked over by the blast.

Of the four bombs dropped by this aircraft, three fell in St Aubyn's playing field. The one which ricocheted from there into Steyning Road destroyed the vicarage but fortunately the vicar and his wife were out shopping and their home help was at the back of the house. It also damaged Maurice Baring's house next door. The second bomb to land in the field bounced over a nearby house and into a garden. It failed to explode and was dealt with by a bomb disposal squad. The third ricocheted and exploded in the grounds of the Tudor House Hotel. Flying glass from a shattered greenhouse cut a gardener on the head and face.

By some miracle, the toll of human life through this raid was slight, with one fatality and seven wounded

The next arrivals in the village were the French Canadians. They moved into the old Tudor Close Hotel and the Preparatory School on the Falmer Road, among other locations. With her mother, Laura Jepson helped to serve them snacks and teas at the canteen that had been set up in the High Street above Miss Tuppen's shop where Dene's Motors now stands.

## A change of priest

The arrival of the French Canadians coincided with a change of priest. In 1942 Father Oswald M Bussy replaced Father James Austin in Rottingdean and soon found that the sheer number of French Canadian worshippers in the village was overtaxing the space available in the convent chapel.

In a letter to Father Cyril Cowderoy he describes his predicament:

> 'I wonder whether it would be possible for me to have faculties for a third Mass on Sundays when necessary, for the troops. At the moment I have over two hundred French Canadians of different units; and yesterday, rightly or wrongly, I used *epikeia** and said a third rather than leave them without Mass. On some Sundays one or other of their own Chaplains will be available if they should remain. I can't say that I am keen on saying three Masses. Two Masses and three talks are more than enough for me for one day. But there are three obstacles to a Supply:
>
> 1 The troops can give me no guarantee from day to day as to whether they will still be here on the day following.
> 2 I have no money to pay a Supply.
> 3 I have no bed to offer him for the night. So, if I can have permission for such occasions as arise I would be most grateful. I certainly can't fit them in at the two regular Masses as they are already crowded with the congregation and the resident troops.'

*Greek for reasonableness. The response to a higher law against the letter of a positive law.

**A post-war postcard of the convent, its chapel and its well-tended vegetable garden.**

It was Father Bussy, no doubt prompted by the severe over-crowding of the convent chapel, who took the momentous decision to have a church built at Rottingdean. On 8 September 1942 he wrote to Father Cowderoy:

> 'Do you think His Grace would have any objection to a future church of Our Lady Queen of Peace in this place? Or, failing that, of Our Lady of Victories? But the latter would sound rather like stealing a march upon the gutted edifice across the Thames. Hence I prefer the former. But I want to make an appeal that will appeal and I don't want to part with Our Lady'.

The appeal for a Thanksgiving Church went ahead. The fact that the church was opened twelve years after the end of the war in no way invalidates Father Bussy's initiative. It was the beginning and foundation of all that followed, albeit in different hands. Sadly, his stay in the village was to be relatively short and he left under a cloud.

☆ ☆ ☆

# 6

# Days of discord

FATHER Oswald Mary Bussy was born in 1902 and ordained on 2 June 1928. In his last year as a seminarian, he was sacristan of the chapel at Wonersh. His first appointment was to Bermondsey. Thereafter, his experience was varied, serving as he did between 1930 and 1941 in Gillingham, Camberwell, East Greenwich, Strood and St Mary Cray. In the latter part of 1941 he was chaplain at the Ursuline convent at Westgate in Kent and the following year he came to this village.

**Father Bussy**

It is regrettable that during the four years that he served in Rottingdean there was dissension and conflict among the parishioners and an antipathy between priest and convent which culminated in his removal to another parish.

The 'facts of the case as they appear to ordinary people' were given 'with little comment and no prejudice' by E M Smith of Arundel Drive, Saltdean in a letter, dated 7 February 1946, to the Bishop of Southwark:

> . . . in February 1945 a Public Servant, the Sub-Post Mistress of Rottingdean, received from the Nuns a letter which accused her of having made in the Post Office, derogatory statements about the Nuns and the running of their school. (I have seen the letter, the statements

were very vague – no doubt Your Grace has also seen the letter).

On the same day, a female member of the Catholic Community rushed into the Post Office when it was full of customers and with all the zeal of the convert, loudly accused the Sub-Post Mistress of having made statements against the Nuns and asking her how she dared, etc. etc. The Sub-Post Mistress could not understand either the letter or this fresh accusation. She refrained, however, from putting the matter in the hands of her Trade Union and asked Father Bussy what it meant.

Father Bussy arranged a meeting between the nuns, the Sub-Post Mistress and the lady to whom the statement had been made. At that meeting it was found that the statement complained of had not been made in the Rottingdean Post Office, but in a distant Post Office, that the statement had nothing to do with the Rottingdean convent, but referred to some convent at a distance. The Sub-Post Mistress received a letter of apology from the nuns and the matter went no further. The Sub-Post Mistress, who is a diabetic, suffered in her health from the attack and unfortunately the whole affair obtained publicity.

The Rottingdean inhabitants were of the opinion that the Sub-Post Mistress had acted with moderation as, if such an accusation could have been proved against her, it would have resulted in her dismissal. Towards the end of 1945, the nuns received an anonymous postcard which no doubt you have seen. I understand that it stated that the chapel was not kept clean and that the convent pupils should return to the convent buildings after Communion in a more orderly fashion . . . One of Father Bussy's penitents, while waiting to make her Confession, actually heard one of the nuns accuse Father Bussy of having written the post card, or alternatively having dictated it to someone and heard Father Bussy answer, without heat, that he knew nothing about it and advised the nuns to think no more about it (the name and address of this person is available). Unfortunately, this advice was not taken and the actual post card seems to have come into circulation in Rottingdean.

One or two members of the Catholic Community appear to have been anxious to find the writer and finally, without inquiry or proof, appear to have fastened the guilt on a member of Father Bussy's household. At any rate the priest's housekeeper, while shopping in the High Street, was loudly attacked by – I regret to say – a member of the Catholic community, who accused her of having written this anonymous post card to the nuns. As in the former incident, this verbal attack in a public place gave the whole incident much publicity.

As it turned out, it was indeed the beleaguered priest's housekeeper who wrote the postcards. She admitted as much with sincere apologies in a letter sent from Oxted on 7 June 1946, stating that she wished to 'withdraw without reserve or condition all that they contained as being untrue'. Sister Veronica, on behalf of the convent, notified Canon Gibney that the apology had been received and that the woman 'had also sent six or seven disgusting cards to a Catholic lady in the village who put the affair in the hands of an expert.'

## A village divided

The matter of the postmistress and the postcard split the village into two camps. Eileen Henessey, writing from her home in Cranleigh Avenue to the Archbishop in November 1945, did not mince her words:

> 'I belong to the oldest Catholic family here in Rottingdean and feel very upset at the way the nuns are treated by the priest. They were the means of bringing the faith to us and helped the beginning of the Catholic Church. They continue to help and provide everything necessary for the upkeep and spread of our religion, and all they get in return are insults from Father Bussy. We, the old inhabitants, feel that something should be done to stop this state of affairs.'

Mrs K M O'Farrell of Chyngton, Steyning Road, was considerably more vehement in her support for Father Bussy. In the first of a series of letters she attacked Archbishop Amigo directly, warning him that it would not be long before he had to give an account of his stewardship.

'What excuse can you possibly make for taking a good fervent Priest (doing splendid work for God) away from such a difficult Parish as Rottingdean?' she asked.

In another letter she accused the archbishop of:

> '. . .destroying something very precious here and leaving us to face the music of all the scandal and gossip in the village about our perfect and most beloved priest.'

Much of her diatribe, however, was directed against the sisters at the convent whom she described as 'a handful of narrow-minded nuns belonging to an almost unknown and certainly negligible Order'.

As one expression of a

## NATION'S GRATITUDE

to Almighty God, whose hand has been so manifestly with us in this War, and to those Sons of Britain and the Empire who have readily sacrificed their all that we might live,

## A THANKSGIVING CHURCH

is to be erected, as soon as it is permissible to do so, by the Catholics of ROTTINGDEAN, SUSSEX, in what has been for so long

## ENGLAND'S FRONT LINE.

Thus will be raised a monument which in the years to come will be a lasting and a living testimony of our gratitude; a monument dedicated to the service of God. And from its altars, long after we ourselves have passed to our reward, will Masses and Prayers continue to be offered to Heaven as a pæan of praise and thanksgiving and a plea for eternal rest for the souls of those whose sacrifice we can never repay.

If you wish to share in this act of homage and gratitude, please send your donations either to :—

Rev. O. M. Bussy, The Priest's House,
Rottingdean, Sussex;

or to The Manager, Westminster Bank,
Rottingdean, Sussex.

---

*"We have one great defect; that is, we forget too easily."*
(Noel Coward, in a Radio Postscript)

The appeal leaflet that caused problems.

A dozen or so letters and four months later Mrs O'Farrell did a U-turn and asked for the archbishop's pardon for writing in the strain she had. She now declared that there was ample proof of the wisdom of his decision to remove Father Bussy 'in increased attendance at weekday Mass and the great increase in Holy Communions'.

## Problems with the appeal

Rottingdean was indeed a difficult parish for Father Bussy. There were even problems with the form of his appeal for funds for the church he wanted to build. Lord Kindersley objected, through Westminster, to 'linking up the National War Savings movement with an appeal for church funds', something he would certainly not have approved had his committee been consulted, as he felt that it should have been. The archbishop, for his part, thought the target of £20,000 too high for a church and a site at Rottingdean, and, what was more, Father Bussy had made the appeal for a national church, not one for a village.

The priest could only reply to the effect that he did not agree that any 'undesirable link' had been formed between the church project and the National Savings Campaign; that £20,000 was not a high figure and the church would be 'national' insofar as the nation would patronise it.

Father Oswald Bussy left Rottingdean at the end of 1945 and moved to All Saints, Oxted, Surrey in January 1946. He died peacefully in Oxted on 18 January 1974 at the age of seventy two, having given nearly thirty years of devoted service to All Saints, one of the most beautiful churches in the diocese. An obituary notice recorded that 'his pastoral zeal was most evident in his loving attention to those who were ill and house-bound.'

☆ ☆ ☆

# 7

# Last years of the convent school

BY June 1949, there were 159 children – 130 non-Catholics – on the books of St Martha's Convent School, a figure which would not be matched again until ten years later. Sixteen of them had made their first Holy Communion and twelve had been confirmed. In 1951/52, the nuns invested £10,000 in extending the school and also began offering accommodation to elderly ladies from the village.

School activities were not limited to term time. The sisters would take groups of pupils on holiday visits to France, often to the Mother House at Périgueux; to a newly-acquired convent in the Pyrenees; and on pilgrimages to Rome.

It was on one such pilgrimage that the headmistress, Sister St Gerard, was killed in a tragic accident. On 13 April 1950 she was accompanying a group of Holy Year pupils and teachers from the convent to Rome, travelling by rail. Another group from the High Barnet convent were making the same journey.

As the train roared through the St Gotthard Tunnel, the headmistress went to investigate a report of water seeping into the corridor from the lavatory compartment and unaccountably opened the door on the wrong side of the train. A young Irish doctor standing in the corridor pulled the communication cord. The nun's severed body was picked up from beside the track twenty five minutes after she fell. Although dead, she was given extreme unction, which is permissible within two hours of a sudden death. Sister St Gerard was taken to the convent in the nearby village of Wassen and was laid out in the chapel. She was buried on Sunday and the children of the village sang at the Requiem Mass.

She had been born Geraldine Cunningham forty five years earlier at Aylrue Hill, Shanahea, Co. Clare, and was the eldest of ten children. She had attended the Convent of St Martha at High Barnet, London and had joined the Order at the age of twenty, entering the novitiate in Périgueux. Sister St Gerard had taught in England for some years before being appointed headmistress.

**Sister St Gerard**

At Sunday Mass, Father Patrick O'Brien paid this tribute to her:

> As a Religious she walked worthy of the vocation to which she was called. She was an exemplary nun, and a great source of edification to all who came her way.
>
> As a teacher of the Catholic faith which was part of her vocation in life, and into which she put her heart and soul together with a tremendous wealth of common sense, I have never in twenty years of fairly varied experience met her equal, and if I did not always take full advantage of all the opportunities for examining the religious knowledge of the children in her care it was in the main an unspoken compliment to Sister St Gerard, in whose teaching I had every reason to have the utmost trust.
>
> I personally feel her loss very much. The community will naturally miss her far more, but the greatest loss will be the children's – both Catholic and non-Catholic – over whose lives and characters she exercised such a wonderful influence for good. It was her goodness and example which attracted so many to the religion which she loved.

In 1958 there was another tragic death. The gardener at the convent, seventy nine year old Percy Cadwallader, committed suicide. He had been slowly losing his sight and, fearing he would be unable to cope alone and blind, he shot himself. Percy, who said he came to Rottingdean from Wales 'and just stayed', had previously been a shepherd and was in charge of the last sheep to graze by the windmill on Beacon Hill.

When Mrs Alex Sloggett, archivist of the Rottingdean Preservation Society, came to live in the village with her husband, Len, in 1955 Percy was still a shepherd. 'At lambing time we used to walk over to the fields near the cricket pitch, where Percy had his lambing pens, and many a time he would give the children a lamb to hold – sometimes it would only be an hour or two old', she said.

It was to be a very long time before the sisters and pupils at both Rottingdean and High Barnet recovered from the most unexpected tragedy that befell Sister St Gerard. However life at the school had to go on and on 11 December 1951 the Diocesan Inspector reported that:

> 'The children of this Junior school, inspected in three groups, showed for the greater part evidence of careful and conscientious instruction. They knew their prayers well, could recite and explain the catechism definitions and were, in the two upper groups, fully conversant with the relevant Doctrine and Scripture. . . Provision was made for the separation of the Infants into two groups for religious instruction.'

The nuns now decided to limit themselves to a junior and infant school. Of the eighty five pupils on the roll, sixty five were girls and

**A 1952 photograph of the seven resident sisters (names in italics) with visitors from other convents.
Back row, l to r: Sisters *Roselyn*, Margaret Mary (Kelly), Cécile, *Bridget Teresa*, Aloysius, Head Teacher *Sister Mary*, Sisters *Mary Pauline*, Margaret Mary and Mary Raphael. Front row: *Sister Veronica*, Mother Cécile, Mother Mary Barnard, Mother Marie de Jésus, Mother M Emmanuel, *Mother Christine*, Mother St Felix, Sister Mary Gertrude and *Sister Avite*.**

there were sixty non-Catholics, forty nine of them girls. The staff were listed as head teacher Sister Mary of the Holy Child assisted by Sister Veronica and Miss N Cronin. There was little change in pupil numbers and composition by July 1953, although the staff had been augmented by Sister Jeanne Elizabeth and Miss J Culley. The report for that year was a highly favourable one:

> 'This little school is doing excellent work for the Catholics of the district. The general standard maintained was most encouraging. There is a splendid spirit here and not only was there evidence that much had been assimilated but the children imparted their knowledge with enthusiasm.'

Subsequent reports were in the same vein:

> **'1954:** These little children acquitted themselves well and maintained a standard throughout that was very good indeed.
> **1955:** These children answered up well and in prayers and doctrine alike maintained a standard that was very good indeed. There is a very happy spirit throughout which reflects great credit upon their teachers.
> **1956:** In spite of having so few Catholic children in the school the standard was remarkably high. In each group there were only four or five children: they are all instructed in separate groups and obviously very great trouble is taken over their religion and the result well repays the efforts. The children take a very great interest in their religion and are well able to talk about it in spite of their youth. Altogether there is a very happy spirit and the good teachers have every reason to feel satisfied with the results of their efforts.
> **1957:** This is a very happy little school. In all the classes the children show a great interest in their religion, and there is plenty of evidence of sound, practical instruction. Prayers, too, are recited devoutly and accurately.'

These reports were produced either by the diocesan inspector or his assistant. In 1958 the examiner was the Reverend F J Walmsley, who wrote in more detail:

> 'In general the state of Religious Education at St Martha's Convent is well up to the standard prevalent throughout the diocese. Prayers were very well known throughout the school. The importance of prayer is inclined to be overlooked, especially among older pupils, but that does not seem to be the case in this school.
> 'Among younger children, knowledge of the catechism was good, and they were eager to answer questions on doctrine. Evidence in plenty of an interest in Christian doctrine, and a desire to make it as attractive as

**Some of the younger pupils all dressed up and ready to entertain.**

possible. The older pupils, being shy, were rather slow to hazard answers. Nevertheless, one's impressions are that they have deep religious convictions even if the majority are either unable or unwilling to put them into words. This reticence to speak on religion is a big drawback among our adults, and therefore every encouragement should be given to these older girls to express themselves, e.g. in discussion and debates. . .'

In 1959/60, a new school magazine was brought out bearing the name Pax. Unfortunately only the first issue is still in the convent's possession. The standard of the contributions is high, as was the case with the publication which appeared a generation earlier.

## Happy – and not so happy – days

Mrs Geraldine Wilson, née Meeson, now living in Hampshire, had such happy memories of her time at the convent that in 1999 she wrote to the *Evening Argus* and the parish newsletter in an attempt to get in touch with her former fellow-pupils. Of her schooldays she says:

St Martha's Convent was a haven for many girls. Being a boarding school and not very expensive it attracted a number of girls whose home lives left rather a lot to be desired. Some of us claimed that we were running away to school because our home lives were unsatisfactory. The nuns were extraordinary in their tolerance and kindness, their dedication to duty and their charity towards some of us whose behaviour was bizarre and often unruly. I had terrible sleep problems suffering from nightmares and sleepwalking so the nuns organised night lights and barriers on the stairs and were the essence of kindness and patience even though they were frequently woken two or three times in any one night.

**A cubicle in one of the dormitories.**

Notwithstanding the demands we made on them we were a very close-knit group. There was a clique of boarders around 1959-61 who banded together. We had midnight feasts, giggling and chatting in the lavatories at the end of the corridors, we shared confidences and being at the age of the most egocentricity we spent endless hours curling our hair with torturous rollers and tucking our skirts up to try and comply with fashion in the outside world.

We were very close to some of the teachers. Miss Moira Anderson (who has since died) was a Miss Jean Brodie figure and Ann Brandford, who died young of cancer, was adored by us all. She taught English and her visionary insights and real feeling for literature ensured we all passed GCE at 'O' and 'A' level and a number of us went on to teach it.

During my time at school I do not never remember any racial tension or bullying. Sometimes someone would be teased but it was all very low key and soon forgotten. There were two Nigerian girls, Donata and Alexandrina. They were cheerful and popular although Donata

**The dining room – 'the food was terrible' says Geraldine.**

suffered dreadfully from chillblains in the winter, so I suppose the heating was not wonderful.

The diet would be frowned on today. It was not unusual for us to have bread, margarine, a rasher of bacon and a spoon of bacon fat for breakfast with the result that we girls were rather overweight. On Wednesdays and Saturdays we would receive a ration from our tuck box. It would consist of two or three sweets, each one handed out with great ceremony by Sister Veronica. I was always rather greedy and watched the box like a hawk to try to assess what my quota would be. Each morning there would be the post and girls received their letters from home. We were not supposed to have letters from anyone other than close family but I got a Valentine once. It was opened in front of the entire assembled school and the words read out in a flat controlled voice by the Reverend Mother, Sister Mary, who succeded in putting me off Valentines forever.

Although the food was terrible and the enclosure something almost unknown today (we didn't go beyond the walls except for a walk on Sundays, from one week to another), we were extremely privileged. The nuns were astonishingly well-read. I was to later get into University on the strength of an interview during which I simply discussed the books which had been available to me at school. The nuns were also extremely good at discussing philosophical and theological issues and one way we managed to go to bed later than our normal bedtimes was by engaging one of them in debate about some obscure theological point. Hours later, and fully elated with the essence of the debate, we would finally be persuaded to our rooms, but emerged the following morning stimulated and inspired to research and continue our discussions. I still have a journal I kept at the age of 17 at school and am astonished by the sophistication of my arguments. . .

We were terribly naughty at times and must have been irksome. Sister Mary Pauline was tried beyond endurance by us. There were rules about having white gloves, hats and white socks for church on Wednesdays and Sundays, when we also had bananas for breakfast! Of course many of us were unable to produce two white gloves when called to do so and much anguish was caused by the knowledge that we were failing to set an example in the village. Once one of the girls threw her hat into the village pond, creating a huge sensation and much speculation on the punishment such an act would attract. I can't remember what happened but suffice to say none of the nuns ever struck us or shouted or swore or lost their tempers. On reflection they really were saints.

Mrs Barbara Cooper (née Owen), now living in Seaford, was a victim of bullying and, as a result, has mixed feelings about her convent days:

I was born in India in 1949 and lived there for five years. When I came to England I lived with my aunt and went to Annecy Convent at Seaford, where the nuns were real disciplinarians, unlike those at St Martha. After a time at Mount St Joseph's in Haywards Heath I went, at the age of eleven, to Rottingdean as a boarder.

My memories of it are not very happy ones as a particular group of girls kept bullying me. It started just after I joined. No action was ever taken, and I never mentioned it, but it did affect me. I hated it and would much rather have been a day girl.

I did make friends, of course. There was Christine Flack, but she was not there for long, and I remember her sisters, Celia and Maureen. Then there was Paula Worth – I went home with her one weekend, which was nice – and the three Carpmale sisters. Renee was the oldest, then Jackie, then Louise. I remember Anthea Taylor and there was Jacqueline Scott, sisters Sharon and Linda Dale, and

Angela Purnell. There were about a dozen boarders and our boarding quarters were in Pax. We had sort of cubicles, individual ones on the first floor, mostly overlooking the gardens. There were long corridors where you used to go to and from the front entrance to the classrooms. The nuns used to sleep at the back of the building. They had classrooms at the back, too, where the gym was, and there was a hall behind Pax.

We used to have tennis matches in the summer just between ourselves on the hard courts. One year we had a match against another school, but I do not remember if we won. There was no hockey but we played netball. For swimming we went down to Rottingdean open-air pool. Every Sunday we went for a walk over the Downs – quite long walks, even as far as Falmer. I used to enjoy them when the weather was nice. Sometimes we would be allowed out into village in our brown uniforms.

In the 1960s, the nuns were faced with changing educational demands and rising costs on all fronts, especially teachers' fees with the revision of the Burnham scale. With reluctance, it was decided that the only option was to close the school. Yet the buildings they had established to the rear of Pax would not be demolished, or even assigned to a different purpose, for before the end of the decade a splendid new voluntary-aided establishment would open on the site.

☆ ☆ ☆

# 8

# Fulfilment of the dream

FATHER Bussy's wartime dream of building a church in Rottingdean became a reality through the drive and tenacity of a priest who took up an embryonic project and saw it through to completion. Father Patrick Joseph O'Brien had, like his predecessor, trained at St John's Seminary in Wonersh, Surrey, and was ordained there in 1930. Before coming to the village he had served a number of parishes in the south, among them Plumstead, Haslemere, Tunbridge Wells and Aylesham, near Canterbury.

**Father Patrick O'Brien**

In that parish, a mining community seven miles south-east of the cathedral city, Father Patrick narrowly missed being killed by the bomb which destroyed his church – a large room attached to a school – and killed thirty four of his neighbours. It shattered a wardrobe in his bedroom and shrapnel was later found in his bed. He was out at the time visiting a sick friend. Had he returned home an hour earlier, events in Rottingdean could have taken an altogether different course.

From Aylesham, Father Patrick served at a church in Northfleet, an industrial town on the Thames west of Gravesend, and from there went to Windlesham, in Surrey. When he arrived in Rottingdean in 1947 he made up his mind to stay. He served the parish for twenty two and a half years, always refusing any larger parishes the bishop might offer him, not only to fulfil his dream but also because he loved living and

**West Strand, now called Nevill House, in Nevill Road.**

working in the village. For nearly a decade, he directed all his energies towards finding a suitable site for a new presbytery and church and raising further funds to add to the £3,291 foundation laid by Father Bussy. With his great devotion to Our Lady of Lourdes, he not only intended to build the church in her honour, but to have it completed in time to celebrate the centenary of the visitations to St Bernadette in 1958. It was an ambition he was to achieve.

His fund-raising efforts yielded substantial results, with help being by no means confined to the parish. Although by 1954 he was still many thousands of pounds short of his target of £16,000, he took the unconventional step of making an appeal for interest-free loans of £100 or less. Surprisingly, this was highly successful.

One property seriously considered for a presbytery was next to The Grange, facing the village pond, but that purchase fell through. Another possible site for a new church was the grass tennis court beside a house called West Strand in Nevill Road. Father O'Brien had lived in it himself for five years after it had been bought by the clergy for £8,500 in July 1948. Before that he had lived in a house named Malvern, in Chailey Avenue.

The majority of the parishioners were, however, against the idea of the church being built on West Strand's tennis court. It was a windy spot and was considered to be quite unsuitable. The plot, which had a frontage of 120 feet and a depth of 170 feet, was bought in 1954 by a building firm, William Willett, and two houses were built on it. One of them, Wave Hill, was bought by Sir Thomas Fyffe Clarke, former Director-General of the Central Office of Information and adviser to Winston Churchill. Fyffe Clarke died there in March 1985.

## Eastfield and its garden

Father Patrick chanced one day on a property which, more than any other, was right in every way for his great plan – a gabled villa in Steyning Road called Eastfield. The large back garden of the house was surrounded by a low flint wall which overlooked an embankment a little way along Whiteway Lane, the old smugglers' track to Saltdean. Nearby stood a group of former shepherds' cottages. This, he decided, was the right place to build his church.

Eastfield had been built in the late nineteenth century by Steyning Beard, who gave his name to the road in which it stands. It was formerly known as Malthouse Lane. The Beard family had lived and owned land in and around the village for many hundreds of years. In the seventeenth century Nicholas Beard would hold meetings at Down House with his fellow Quakers. His refusal to pay tithes resulted in an on-going feud with the Reverend Robert Baker, vicar of St Margaret's from 1627 to 1679, and in his imprisonment on a number of occasions. Steyning Beard, who died in 1910, was the Master of the Brookside Harriers. The pack, which was kennelled just north of Dean Court Road, consisted of some twenty five couples of crossbred harriers and were hunted over about ten square miles of downland and arable country around the village.

There was, however, one major problem to overcome in respect of Eastfield – the then owners, Mr Pitchford and his daughter, did not wish to sell it. They remained adamant, despite all Father O'Brien's entreaties and offers.

It was many months before there was any further development, but when it occurred it was dramatic. One day Mr Pitchford telephoned to say that his son was about to take a course at an agricultural college

**Eastfield in Steyning Road, Rottingdean. The site for the new church was the large garden at the back.**

and he thought that it might be beneficial if they could buy a house with a substantial amount of adjoining land. Was Father O'Brien still interested in Eastfield?

What followed is history. One can only guess at the joy in the priest's heart now that he knew for certain that his vision could be realised.

## Neighbours complain

When the site had been purchased and outline planning permission obtained, and with funds coming in from various sources, the project hit a major setback. Neighbouring householders objected to the proposed church's tower, claiming that it would overshadow their gardens. It took the thoughtful use of an electric torch – and a public inquiry – to persuade them that it would not.

Mrs Winifred K Russell of Corner House, Rottingdean, a house close to the site, was the first to complain about the height of the proposed tower. She wrote to Brighton's Town Clerk on 22 May 1954 saying that she had already signed a petition against the plan to build a church on the site but now felt she should also send this personal appeal:

> 'My house, which I purchased in August, 1952, is next door to Eastfield on the west side. My family and I occupy the ground floor. Most of my windows face east and the house is flush with the rather narrow twitten separating the two houses, so that the erection of any large building in the next garden must of necessity make my rooms very dark.
>
> 'As it is, they are not by any means light rooms, but I can see the sky and the treetops. I dread the thought of a large building in that lovely garden shutting out the light and air. I think the majority of people would answer 'no' if the proposal related to their own next-door garden. It will quite destroy our view and the feeling of airiness and space, and in my opinion will definitely detract from the value of the adjoining properties.
>
> 'The local Catholics want their own church, but please, not in one of the gardens.'

She followed this up on 11 October with a letter to Miss Jessie Seymour, secretary of the Rottingdean Ratepayers' Association and Preservation Society of which she was a member, expressing the view that Eastfield's garden was 'an unsuitable and undignified spot for a church.' Indeed, a friend of hers had said that it would look like 'a hen sitting on a basin':

Her letter goes on:

> 'Personally I would not have used that simile, but I do know exactly what he meant. A church built in an already built-up area will be entirely out of place.
>
> 'I object to the ringing of their bells, which I can already hear quite plainly from the convent. I object to the increase of traffic which must ensue, and which will quite spoil the corner between the library and the proposed church entrance. (We heard the priest pointing out to some friends where the entrance is to be).
>
> 'More than anything else I object to the amount of light it will shut out from my flat, which is quite dark enough already, being on the ground floor. . . I think it was extremely ungenerous of them [the council] to grant this permission before consulting other interested parties.
>
> 'If they wanted a church on the level and close to the convent, why did they not buy the site now known as Timbers, which was on the market for months? Why do they not buy the Boys' Club, on Falmer Road, which I hear is for sale? I cannot understand how they can wish to build their church in a position which so many people find objectionable.'

Her objections, and those of the owners of other adjacent properties,

**Site clearance work in progress in the garden of Eastfield.**

had been upheld by the council on 27 July 1954. Its planning committee rejected the detailed plans that had been submitted because it considered the tower of the church was 'too high having regard to its close proximity to the adjoining houses'.

A second application showing the whole building at a lower level than the original application to the extent of about 5ft was considered in April 1955. Again the committee turned it down because it was still not satisfied that the height of the tower would not be detrimental to the adjoining residences.

On 17 May a revised application, with the proposed tower completely omitted, was considered. The committee, 'satisfied that the applicant had done everything which could reasonably be asked for in order to meet the objections which had been raised', recommended the council to approve the scheme.

Mrs Russell continued to express strong feelings on the matter and her words were interpreted by some local government officers as a direct attack on Catholics in Rottingdean. Their own response was, in retrospect, rather heated since the front page of the *Sussex Daily News* of

3 February 1956 carried a report in which the people of Rottingdean were accused of 'hateful bigotry' in their objections to the erection of the church in Steyning Road.

Mrs Russell responded the same day to the effect that:

> 'Everyone whom I have talked to has deplored the building as a building but not one of them has spoken against the church. Most of the residents of Steyning-road are members of St. Margaret's church (C. of E.) and I would like Councillor FitzGerald and Alderman Cullen – who supported him – to know that bigotry and intolerance are not part of our religion. Some of us in Steyning-road are still in communication with the Ministry of Housing and Local Government in Whitehall. We are trying to find out why the preliminary planning permission was given before we were notified of the intention to build a large church in the garden of a house in an already built-up area. . .'

Father O'Brien had, for his part, lodged an appeal against Brighton Corporation's refusal to grant permission to add a tower to the church, which by then was nearing completion.

At the ensuing public inquiry he produced a petition in support signed by 300 people, many of them non-Catholics. His architect, Henry Towner, produced a torch and a scale model of the proposed church and the surrounding properties. With the light from the torch he demonstrated the week-by-week position of the sun and the length and direction of its shadows. He was able to show that the shadows cast by the proposed tower would fall on the gardens bordering the site for only a short period in the evenings of high summer and they would fall only on the patches of shade from the trees in the gardens. The demonstration demolished the opposition and the plans went through without any more hitches.

## The church's architect

Henry Towner not only drew up the plans for the church, and resolved the issue of the shadows from the tower at the inquiry, but also advised on all the building's fixtures and fittings. He personally designed the votive candle stands, which were made in Uckfield, and the six candlesticks on the High Altar which were produced in Wellingborough. The High Altar itself was copied from that of a church in Segovia.

Henry Bingham Towner (1909-1997) was born in Uckfield and was educated at the Xaverian College in Brighton and later Mayfield College with the intention of becoming a priest. He decided, much to his mother's regret, that he was not suited for the church and went to Brighton College to study structural engineering.

**Henry Towner.**

After qualifying he decided to take an architectural course at Brighton Art School and, when he had completed it successfully, he joined an architectural practice in London. In 1937, at the age of twenty eight, he took a job in Warwick to get experience of a country practice before returning to Sussex to start up on his own.

At the outbreak of war he joined the Royal Engineers Survey, first serving in the UK. His bride-to-be, Dana, was in the ATS, working at GHQ with him in London for a short time. They married in 1942, shortly before Henry was posted to West Africa to survey the route of a possible road from Accra to Khartoum.

After the war he resumed his practice in Uckfield, specialising in churches, mostly Catholic. He designed more than twenty five in the years he was in practice, usually either in flint or stone. St Wilfred's at Hailsham was his first church and among those that followed were: St Francis of Assisi, Moulsecoomb, which was re-opened 1969; Holy Rood, Pevensey Bay; St Joseph's, Milford; Christ the King, Langley; St Thomas of Canterbury, Mayfield; St John Vianney, Bexley Heath; St Teresa of Avila, Chiddingfield; St Gabriel, Billingshurst; Central Worthing church and its convent school; the church at East Worthing; an addition to abbey ruins at Reading (St James); St Mark's Church, West Wickham; St Thomas More, Patcham; churches at Burnham and Chelmsford and the Church of the Holy Family, Lancing. He was also responsible for the reconstruction of numerous old buildings, and new houses built of traditional local materials.

## Craftsmen at work

The church took eighteen months to build, and the entire construction work was carried out by only five craftsmen under the direction of Robert William Moppett and his brother, Leslie Frederick Moppett. The principal building material was flint – the stone used for so many of Rottingdean's buildings – and the builders were fortunate enough to engage the services of the last full-time flintworker in the district. So workmanlike was the construction of the church that neither its architect nor any visiting builders could find a single defect in it at any stage, or on completion.

Perhaps the most remarkable feature of the church was not a visible or tangible one – it was the fact that the sum of £25,000 was collected over a period of only three years, enabling the building to be consecrated the year after it was opened. The money came from within and outside the parish, in sums ranging from a few shillings to one of £3,000.

Much of it was offered as loans, although in every case the lender later told Father O'Brien to keep it. An eighty year old pensioner

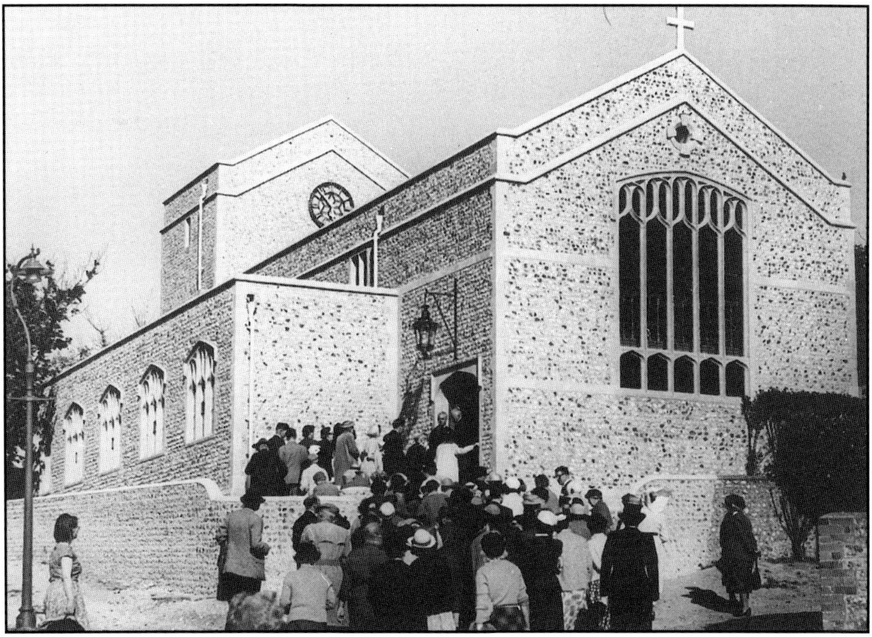

**Parishioners queue for admission to the first service in the new church.**

**Father O'Brien conducts the first Solemn High Mass.**

offered £100. Father Patrick suggested she had better make it a loan since she might one day need it herself. No, she replied, she would give it, although she did ask him to pay her funeral expenses should she die before she could save up enough to meet them. She did, in fact, have enough for her last needs and, in addition, made a further gift to the church.

## The first Solemn High Mass

Thursday, 13 June 1957 was a day of great personal joy for both Father O'Brien and his parishioners, a large proportion of whom were from Saltdean and other outlying communities. The building was filled to overflowing, with those who had queued being admitted forty minutes before the service began.

Assisted by Father Edward O'Connor of Wandsworth as deacon and Father Waugh of Haywards Heath as sub-deacon, both of whom were seminary classmates, Father Patrick celebrated the first Solemn High Mass in his new church. In the Sanctuary with them was Monsignor Clement Constable, Dean of Brighton and parish priest of the Church of the Sacred Heart, Hove. Many other clergy who were both friends and neighbours were present, including Father Patrick's predecessor in Rottingdean, Father Oswald Bussy.

Father Arthur Flanagan of St John the Baptist, Kemp Town, who had always helped and encouraged Father O'Brien in his endeavours, was asked by him to preach on this occasion and he chose as his theme the history of the parish and the great efforts which were being crowned on that day. The Mass ended with the packed congregation standing and singing the familiar Lourdes hymn, *Ave, Ave Maria,* and with the blessing of the new church.

After the service many of the people present took the opportunity to examine the interior of the church and its fixtures and fittings.

An item that aroused great interest was the icon which adorns the wall on the epistle side. It had been presented to Father O'Brien by Father Flanagan who had himself obtained it when on a visit to northern Russia. Its frame is of gold on silver and it shows, in exquisite detail, Our Lady holding the Child Jesus.

**The icon on the wall on the epistle side is believed to be from the village of Hiborla, near Moscow.**

The Stations of the Cross had each been carved by craftsmen in Italy from one solid piece of wood at a cost of £32 10s (£32.50). Other wooden fittings include the oak altar rails donated by a parishioner, oak seating crafted in Wivelsfield and a teak spiral staircase.

In the two side chapels there are two permanent stone altars and statues, sculpted from Carrara marble, of the Sacred Heart and Our Lady of Lourdes respectively. The altars and font were made at the

**The High Altar with its carved baldachin and the candlesticks designed by Henry Towner.**

workshops of the Guild of St Joseph and St Dominic, Ditchling. Kenneth Eager, later to be the head of that establishment, was responsible for all the lettering in the church – a predecessor of his and co-founder of the Guild, Eric Gill, is perhaps best known for his stone carvings of the Stations of the Cross for Westminster Cathedral.

A little to the left of the pulpit stands a carved wooden figure of St Joseph, axe in hand. The power of prayer to St Joseph should not be under-estimated – witness the effect of the Novena called for by Father Dreves when seeking a site for a new chapel and Father Mc Sheehy's experience when two large candlesticks were stolen from the church in 1984. On the feast of St Joseph the priest said to him 'Today is your feast; how about celebrating it by finding our candlesticks?' After Mass, a CID officer arrived with them under his arm. They had been found on a dump in Brighton.

Above the High Altar is an imposing yet simple carved baldachin, or canopy. The carving round it is from South Park, originally part of the great park of Penshurst Place, near Tunbridge Wells, where in 1554 Sir Philip Sydney was born. South Park had been enormously improved and modified by Henry Hardinge, created Viscount Hardinge of Lahore in 1848 after a four year spell as Governor-General of India. When it was sold to a development company in 1956 it consisted of five reception rooms, sixteen bedrooms and six bathrooms. The house was demolished and its magnificent 147 acre site, commanding views across the rolling countryside, cleared for the construction of new dwellings. Almost at once it was realised that, in heritage terms, this had been a disastrous mistake. An attempt was made to re-erect the mansion, but the cost proved prohibitive and in any event only a portion of the attempted re-constructiom was successful.

A mere £1,300 was realised at the demolition sale of fittings and equipment from South Park. The whole of the carved oak panelling in the library, reputed to date from the fifteenth and sixteenth centuries, was sold for £38 and an Indian cupboard, with carved and copper-covered doors, fetched £50.

Among the external fittings purchased from South Park for the new church at Rottingdean were the double front doors and a flat-bed gravity escapement turret clock which had been built in 1854, the year Big Ben was completed, by Thomas Cooke of York. Norwich and Durham cathedrals both originally had clocks by Cooke.

The clock from South Park was, however, not installed in the tower of the church at Rottingdean but was sold, which is a pity, since today it would be an object of extreme rarity and great value.

Instead an electrically-operated clock was bought from Smith's of London, a firm which can trace its pedigree back to the eighteenth century. According to the late Florence Hulme, Father O'Brien would have preferred a chiming clock but the chimes would have clashed with those of nearby St Margaret's church. The complete overhaul the clock needed recently has been paid for by a local benefactor.

The bell in the church loft above the main altar was made by J Warner and Sons, Crescent Works Foundry, London and dates from 1853. It is another of the treasures from South Park. The same maker produced, in the following year, one of the three bells of the Betteshanger church of St Mary. Lying on the loft floor of the church at

Rottingdean are the old bell clapper and the original fittings. The new clapper was at some stage fitted with a solenoid so the bell could be operated electrically. Through the generosity of the same parishioner who paid for the overhauling of the clock, the bell has been restored.

## The organ – a bargain buy

The organ was an absolute bargain. Henry Towner secured it at auction for £50. He had initially offered the South Park demolition contractors £250, but they preferred to auction it. The instrument had been made in 1858, coincidentally the year of the Lourdes apparitions, by J W Walker and Sons of Suffolk for Lady Hardinge, and was one of four similar ones produced around that period.

The resident organist at Penshurst, Anthony Brockhurst, has details of the specifications of church organs throughout Kent and Sussex. The organ here was one he had not yet seen and he was delighted to be given an opportunity to come and examine it. He reported that the instrument was certainly interesting and, for its date, in excellent playing condition. Although made in the same year as the one in the church at Penshurst, it was quite different in that it was built as a chamber organ for house use.

It was typical of its type and date. The pedal board had an octave and a half of pedals, but had pipes only from low C to B above, the remainder being coupled to the manual. Many of the stops were to tenor C only and a common bass served them all. A 16 foot pedal bourdon was coupled to the lower octave on the manual in order that the organ could be played effectively by a player unable to use the pedal board – in effect, a sort of melodic bass.

All pipework except, he believed, the bourdon pipes, was contained within the swell box. It was beautifully voiced and of superior quality. The front display pipes were wooden and did not speak.

'All told it is a gem of an instrument', said Anthony Brockhurst. 'But any ideas of enlarging it or adding to the specification would almost certainly be disallowed by faculty because of the instrument's historical significance. Grants would only be forthcoming if it were to be restored exactly as it was, using authentic period materials'.

Although all the various items added £3,000 to the cost of the church, they blended in perfectly with its general design and served as a tribute to the architect who had secured so many of them.

## The church is consecrated

Within fifteen months or so of its completion the church was free of all debt. Through subscriptions from parishioners, the amount of £23,000 had been paid in full.

On Wednesday 10 September 1958, Our Lady of Lourdes was consecrated by the Bishop of Southwark, the Right Reverend Cyril Cowderoy, in a ceremony attended by more than forty priests from local parishes. The proceedings, with Mass, lasted about five hours. Large numbers of parishioners and crowds of holidaymakers watched as the bishop blessed the outside of the building by sprinkling holy water on the walls. He then entered the church with his attendants and the choir of priests, followed by the general public. The first part of the ceremony inside the church consisted of declarations and responses, with the bishop and the rest of the congregation kneeling.

The singing by the clergy and choir echoed through the building, calling to mind the chanting of monks in the Middle Ages. The bishop then traced the Greek and Jewish alphabets in sand, small heaps of which had been placed in a pattern on the floor. By using the crozier in this way he symbolised the Jews and Gentiles. He then consecrated the High Altar and anointed the twelve Consecration Crosses on the walls of the church with oil.

The consecration ceremony was followed by Pontifical High Mass, in which Father O'Brien assisted. The organist was Brother Cagetan of the Xaverian College in Brighton.

## Some 'firsts' in the new church

On 5 September 1957, the first couple to be married in the new church took their vows. Edmund Smith was a veterinary surgeon and his bride, Mary Crane, was a sister at the Sussex Eye Hospital in Eastern Road, Brighton.

Mary had converted to the faith in 1954 and usually attended services at St John the Baptist, Kemp Town, which was conveniently near the hospital where she worked. However, as her family home was in Eley Drive, Rottingdean, Our Lady of Lourdes' became her parish church. Edmund had worked in Jarvis Brook, near Crowborough for three years and in 1947 set up on his own account, moving to Andover in Hampshire, where they are still based.

**The first wedding group to pose for photographs outside Our Lady of Lourdes.**

In September 1997, they returned to Rottingdean to celebrate forty years of marriage, having made arrangements beforehand with Father Charles Jeffries to visit the church. To their surprise and delight, they arrived to find a congregation of thirty five or so parishioners who had come to wish them well. They attended Mass at precisely the same time, and stood at exactly the same spot, as they had all those years earlier. A buffet had been laid on for them in the parish room and they were presented with flowers. Edmund and Mary have six children, of whom two are in the USA, two in the North of England, one in the Midlands and one in Cardiff.

Rottingdean resident John G Hale was among the members of the congregation in 1957 and his late wife, Bettie, was the first convert after the building of the church. His late father, Sylvester Gresham Hale, died in October that year when in Rottingdean visiting his family from his native New Zealand. The last rites were given in an apartment in St Margaret's Flats next to his family's and his was the first Requiem Mass to be held at Our Lady of Lourdes. His body was then shipped back to Hamilton, North Island, New Zealand, for interment.

The parish returns of 11 August 1958 show that in the previous year there had been eight baptisms of children under the age of fourteen and four of converts. The last baptism in the convent had been that of one Teresa Chisholm on 17 April 1957. The first in Our Lady of Lourdes was that of Loretta Sandra Moss of 4 Donnington Road, Woodingdean, on 16 September 1957, with Father Edward O'Brien officiating. Next was Christine Mary Turner, the daughter of Brian and Ann, who was born on 7 August and baptised on 20 October by Father Thomas B Kearns. Brian Turner was a non-Catholic at the time and converted in 1966 in what was, in restrospect, a very low key affair. It consisted of a declaration of faith followed by the sacrament of penance. Only his wife and Father Patrick O'Brien were present. One of the earliest to make their First Holy Communion in the church was John Boon, on the feast of Corpus Christi. He continues to be one of the stalwarts of the choir.

## The only ordination – so far

The ordination of the Turners' son, Paul, on 7 May 1989 was the first – and has so far been the only – one to have taken place in the church of Our Lady of Lourdes. Paul was born in Rottingdean in 1960 and served as an altar boy at the church from the age of seven until he left home at eighteen. He gained a degree in business studies at Middlesex Polytechnic, working for a time as an accounting clerk as part of his degree course. He then spent a year as a trainee retail manager and during that time realised that he was being called to the priesthood. He gained a degree in theology at St John's Seminary, Wonersh which was validated by Southampton University. Following his studies he spent ten months as a deacon at Crawley.

Paul was very much in the public eye on the occasion of the Renew celebration held at Brighton and Hove Albion's Goldstone ground. Here, on 25 September 1988, more than 16,000 Catholics from parishes all over Sussex gathered for an open-air Mass celebrated by Bishop Cormac. Paul, then a deacon, was among those attending on the bishop and stood next to him as he lit the symbolic flame to start the service. A recorded message from the Pope was played and a 'plane flew over the ground trailing a Renew banner.

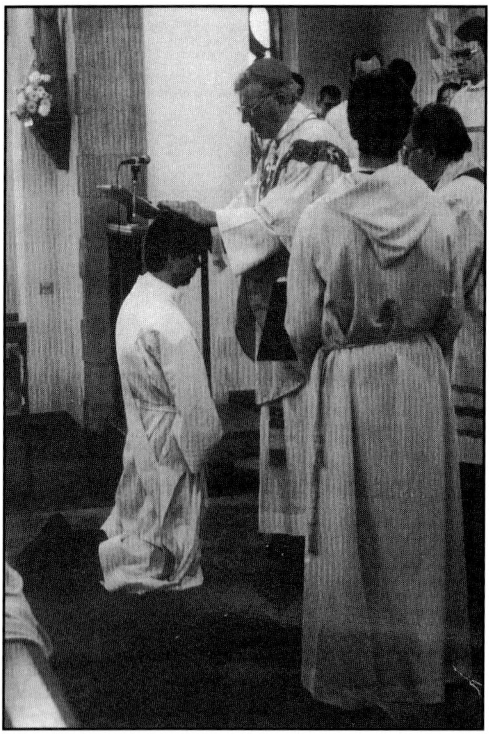

**Paul is ordained at Our Lady of Lourdes.**

Priests of the diocese joined the bishop in conducting prayers and went into the stands to give communion. Hundreds of schoolchildren took part in a march past, waving banners.

Similar programmes were being held at the same time in America, Australia and South Africa with the object of refreshing people's spiritual lives and goodwill messages from those countries were read out to the crowds.

The following year, Paul was presented for ordination by Father McSheehy. The church was packed for the

**Father Paul officiates at his sister's wedding.**

occasion and the atmosphere was like a great family gathering. Afterwards there was a reception at the Whiteway Centre, and in the evening three dozen or so members of the family and close friends had a meal at the Coach House.

The next day, a Monday, Father Paul celebrated his first Mass here in his own parish church, and he said that he found it 'more nerve-wracking than the ordination itself.' Following tradition a fellow priest was there to help him – Father Paul Maddison, a seminary friend from the East Anglian diocese, delivered the sermon for him, so he was at least spared that worry.

Just a month after his ordination Father Paul performed his first wedding ceremony at Our Lady of Lourdes. The bride was his sister, Susan, and she was married to Bryan Lawrence from Dundee.

☆ ☆ ☆

The southern elevation of the Church of Our Lady of Lourdes.

The wedding of the author's sister, Anna, to Christopher Dickens attracted much media attention for the bride belonged to one of Italy's oldest noble houses.

# 9

# Consolidation

FATHER Patrick O'Brien was immensely proud of his new church, and rightly so. Those were the days when a number of parishioners, my own family included, would walk to the church along the rough track known familiarly as Whiteways. It led from the west of inland Saltdean, where at that time many of the roads were unmade and turned to rivers of mud and chalk in a wet winter. More than once, Father O'Brien would be heard from the pulpit asking parishioners not to enter the building with dirty shoes.

There is little comparison between the relationship a parish priest now has with his congregation and that which prevailed some forty years ago. Then there were no friendly conversations in the porch after Mass, hardly any formal or informal meetings to discuss parish policies and little involvement by the priest in village life. Indeed, there was a distinctly anti-Catholic attitude in Rottingdean in those days and this seemed to prevail for at least a decade. Of ecumenism there was hardly any sign.

According to the Southwark Visitation Form of 7 May 1958 the last parish census had been made in March 1950 by Father O'Brien himself on a house-to-house basis and a census was currently being conducted. It revealed that some fifteen different families were visited each month and on average each family was visited twice a year. The priest was helped by the religious in his parish through the teaching in their private school, and boys and girls who had left school were kept in touch with the church through him visiting the families. Concerning what was being done in the parish to bring about the conversion of non-Catholics, Father O'Brien reported 'at the moment – nothing.'

As far as holidays were concerned, he said he did take an annual one but otherwise left the parish 'very seldom'. This situation changed a few years later, when he was away with increasing frequency.

Father O'Brien retired in June 1968 and he was wished 'God Speed' by the *Rottingdean Church and Parish News* on behalf of the local Anglican community:

> 'We shall miss the twinkle in his eye, but know for sure that he will have Rottingdean always in his heart.'

By that time, he would have been in Holy Orders for thirty eight years, two-thirds of them spent in the village. He died in Spain in 1974.

## Father John Grant 1968-1972

Father John Waldron Grant was born on 11 June 1916 at Norbury, London and educated by the Jesuits at Wimbledon College. He entered St John's Seminary, Wonersh, where he was ordained in 1946. From 1946 to 1951 he served as assistant priest at Woking, a place where he was delighted to live as he had a great interest in railways. He then joined the teaching staff at St Joseph's College at Mark Cross.

**Father Grant**

In a letter dated 13 May 1968 confirming Father Grant's appointment to Rottingdean, Bishop Cashman observed: 'There is much to be done and . . . the parish has great promise if handled rightly.'

There was no formal induction ceremony. Instead Father Grant had to make a Profession of Faith to his Dean, Canon Fincham, and return a document testifying to the diocese that he had formally taken over the parish. Although the bishop had been anxious to try and induct all newly appointed priests in his area, he had had to abandon the idea and his good resolution largely as a result of his health and the number of inductions which would be necessary. Several parish priests along the coast, eg. St Peter's Hove, Portslade, Southwick and Shoreham, had similarly been dispensed from a formal induction ceremony a short time before. For his part, Father Grant deemed the new arrangement 'a much simpler process.'

He moved to Rottingdean on 26 June 1968, but still had to return to his old college two or three times a week to ease his successor's takeover until the end of term. Mrs Rosemary Reade, who first came to this parish in 1965, and the late Phyllis Chinn, helped him settle into the presbytery until such time as his aged mother, Carmel, was able to move in with him. She became his housekeeper here and when he was appointed to a post in Arundel, she naturally went with him. He acquired a dog, a Labrador named Judy, which grew to a substantial size.

Father Grant started the parish council during his time here and managed to tidy up the parish finances. In this he was helped by the bishop, to whom he wrote in September 1968:

> 'I was very pleased and relieved to hear from Father Stonehill yesterday that you had authorised him to write off the £1,560 owing from this parish to the Diocesan Deanery Fund for past years. It would have been impossible to tackle this debt for some time, and it would have remained a nasty, heavy cloud on the horizon, which you have very kindly dispersed. I am most grateful.'

It was during his tenure that the first stirrings of local ecumenism began to be seen. In 1968 St Martin's Presbyterian church and the Anglican parish church of St Nicholas at Saltdean had formed an Inter-Church Committee. In June it suggested to Father Grant that he join in a Unity Week service. He, in turn, wrote to the bishop:

> 'The Vicar of Saltdean has asked me to preach in his church on 19 January at a Unity Week Service. I have pointed out that it is very unlikely that he will get an invitation to preach in mine, but he doesn't mind. He wants to have – at last – some Catholic participation in what previously has always been an Anglican-Presbyterian affair. I have told the vicar that I would accept if the bishop gives me permission.'

## Ecumenical links

In the event, the first local three-way service was held at St Nicholas' church in the context of a week of prayer for Christian unity. It was conducted by the vicar, the Reverend Derek Tansill, and the minister of St Martin's, the Reverend D Alisdair Pratt. Father Grant preached, and the music was provided by the Brighton Salvation Army Band.

Representatives of the three churches met again at St Martin's in

November 1970 to discuss ways of increasing co-operation between all the churches in the area. It was decided that a joint Christmas card should be produced each year and this has become an established practice. A joint magazine was to come later. The idea had first been raised in June 1969 but not until November 1973 was a sub-committee of the Saltdean Churches Committee formed to consider the matter. Agreement in principle had been reached between the two Saltdean churches by the following May, although Our Lady of Lourdes, by that time in the care of Father Cyril Butler, did not initially lend its support to the scheme. Work went ahead with the venture nevertheless, and the magazine, bearing the name *LINK*, made its first appearance in January 1976. It was immediately successful, and remains so. Our Lady of Lourdes has had its own section in the publication for many years and it also contributed to the *Rottingdean Church and Parish News* for a time.

Father Grant evidently found he had more than enough to do for on 14 November 1969 he put in a bid for a deacon, but without success, the bishop replying to the effect that the only one available was being assigned to Woking for his experimental period in a parish.

The priest was popular among many of his parishioners, although he never lost a somewhat professorial manner. A meticulous man, precise in his movements – he had worked in a bank before becoming a priest – he was a perfectionist and a little impatient. A tell-tale sign to the altar servers and congregation was the tapping of one foot. In extreme cases, the altar missal would be banged down.

He recognised dedication to the church, on one occasion presenting Mrs Anne Joy (then Mallinson) with a vase for all the work she had put into arranging flowers. Another helper, Mrs Molly Taylor, recalled that he liked the flowers to match his vestments. He involved parishioners in church affairs – witness the new parish council. When the encyclical *Humanae Vitae* was published, he called a meeting for a full and frank discussion on the contentious subject of birth control. He dutifully, and with no show of reluctance, complied with liturgical and other changes in forms and procedures imposed by his ecclesiastical superiors.

Following his four years in Rottingdean, Father Grant took on the high-profile post of administrator and Canon of Arundel Cathedral until September 1978. His last parish was at Hailsham and from there, in 1991, he retired to St Anne's Convent, Burgess Hill. He died on 1

September 1994 at St Francis' Nursing Home, Littlehampton, at the age of seventy eight.

## The choir

The choir was Father Grant's legacy to the parish. It was formally established in 1968, and originally consisted of altos Jenny Walsh (leading), Phyllis Chinn, Christine Turner and Joanna Kent; sopranos Milly Hawkins, Cecilia Beard, Zita McCauley, Peg Middlemas and Sheila Woodman; tenors Bert Middlemas and John Boon; and bass Syd Ward and Arthur 'Bill' Waine.

Anne Allinson, who was to conduct it for fourteen years, came to Rottingdean at the end of 1969 when, as she recalls:

> 'Father Grant was still training the choir and conducting it from the altar with his eyebrows. He had good taste in music and his discipline was strict. Any mistakes were greeted with obvious signs of displeasure. Apart from cathedrals and a few isolated churches like Brompton Oratory, there was no tradition of well-trained choirs in Catholic parishes as there is in the Anglican church. People joined the choir because they

**Organist Philip Stephens, centre in a white shirt, with Anne Allinson beside him in the right foreground, pictured with the choir in December 1990.**
*Photo: Anne Allinson.*

**A decade later – the choir in the gallery on 13 February 2000. L to r: Peter Woodman, John Boon, Marisa Craig, Ann Knox, Heather Caffrey, Philip Stephens, Frances Reidy, Natalie Lepri, Huguette Vincent and Sheila Woodman.** *Photo: John Knox*

volunteered. They were not auditioned as a rule and very few could read music. There were those who sang flat or sharp, who wobbled or grated but nothing could be done. One woman sang because she found it did her asthma good and another refused to sing the hymns if Wesley had composed them because he wasn't a Catholic . . .

'Fred Hopkins, who joined the tenors later, was conducting the choir by 1974. In those days it had two basses, three tenors, three or four altos and about seven sopranos. Apart from three plainsong Masses, various four part Latin Masses were sung. These were of the florid type. Some had many repetitions and were really choir performances with no participation from the congregation.

'Father Butler, a traditional Latinist, was parish priest at that time. He was totally opposed to united services and also to folk groups. He once expressed the view that if guitar players were allowed into the church, you would find him in the Anglican church – and that was strong language for him. There were nevertheless a few English Masses e.g. Dom Gregory Murray and the choir sang a motet at the Offertory. These were mostly Latin, although Father Grant had introduced one or two English motets by composers like Elgar and Vaughan Williams.'

The choir's Music Fund Book records an opening balance, in 1972, of £2.60 representing collections from members. The main source of income thereafter was weddings and funerals, when £5 or more was given. Main debit items were the purchase of music and photocopying costs. The choir paid for itself until mid-1998, when Father Charles Jeffries offered to take responsibility for its finances.

## A Folk Group and Folk Masses

Three of Mrs Ann Turner's Children – Stephen, who played guitar, flautist Susan, and vocalist Karen, who also played guitar and cello – had gained valuable experience in leading the Liturgy at the Church of St Louis of France at Whitehawk and this gave her the confidence in 1979 to suggest to Father McSheehy, when he became parish priest, that they might play at Rottingdean. He readily agreed and it was decided that the first time the group would play at a Mass would be in the convent chapel on a Saturday evening, which at the time was an extra Mass to the usual Sunday Liturgy.

'I was not sure how guitars, flutes, cellos would be received in

**The Folk Group and its founder. Back row: Mrs Ann Turner, Christine McCabe, Claire McCabe and Karen Turner. Front row: Linda Cassidy, Nicola Pierce, Stephen Turner, Susan Turner and Tom McInerney.**

Rottingdean and fully expected that the only people to attend the Mass would be the parents of the children taking part, and the nuns', said Ann Turner. 'But in fact the chapel was full to overflowing and more than one person asked why the folk group could not play in the church for one of the regular Masses.

'This was all the encouragement we needed and for a time we played at an occasional 10.15am Mass. This soon settled into a Folk Mass once a month and was well supported by the congregation. The group also became responsible for organising the Liturgy for the First Communion Mass and we invited the choir to join us for that occasion. Eventually we also joined in the Christmas Midnight Mass and played carols at the next Mass on Christmas morning. Father McSheehy always presented us with a large tin of sweets at the Christmas morning Mass, which we shared with all the children in the church and some of the adults too'.

When her children left home to go to college or university, Ann found it difficult to keep the folk group going. She was not a musician herself and relied on her son, Stephen, and daughters Susan and Karen, to arrange the music. The last time they played in Our Lady of Lourdes was on 8 May 1989, on a very special occasion for the family – the first Mass of their brother, Father Paul Turner, who had been ordained the day before.

## Songs of Praise

For the choir and its conductor, Anne Allinson, 1980 was a particularly eventful year. In February it was invited to take part in the recording of *Songs of Praise* in St Peter's church, Brighton. In September, Radio Brighton recorded Mass from Rottingdean for the first time, the choir coming down into the body of the church to sing Thompson's short Mass in Latin. Later that year Our Lady of Lourdes choir sang for Confirmation in the cathedral at Arundel with another small choir and in November took part in the first choir festival held there.

In our own parish, more English Masses were introduced and the more florid Latin Masses were phased out. Congregational copies of all the English Masses were made so that there could be full participation, a new hymn book was bought to afford a wider choice and many more motets and carols were added to the repertoire.

The choir became affiliated to the Royal School of Church Music and has a certificate signed by its director, Dr Lionel Dakers, hanging in the gallery. This certificate records that the Church of Our Lady of Lourdes 'has undertaken to do its best to promote the cause of good Church Music' and that choirs and organists are 'the responsible leaders of the congregation in all that they do, and by their action should show reverence and devotion'.

Masses and hymns on special occasions were sometimes chosen by a parishioner and if there was a fifth Sunday in the month Father McSheehy would reserve the right to choose the hymns himself. He even went to the extent of setting up a Liturgy Committee but it only existed for a year, after which Anne Allinson returned to doing all the planning as before.

When Father McSheehy decided that all the carols before Midnight Mass should be sung by the congregation, instead of alternately by congregation and choir as in previous years, Anne introduced a carol service on one of the Sundays before Christmas. It initially took the form of nine lessons and carols and it gave the choir an opportunity to introduce new carols, some in German and French.

Anne conducted a last carol service in 1990 before moving with her husband to Dorset.

'Afterwards there was a wonderful party in the convent with most generous presentations from the parish and the choir' she recalled. 'The choir sang me a very amusing song set to the tune of one of my least favourite folk hymns. I was very sad to leave them all, but I did leave behind a legacy of much new music and sound training which they have continued to use in my absence. In Father McSheehy we were especially fortunate to have a priest who appreciated music, sang well himself and was very conscious of the contribution that music makes to the dignity and reverence of the ceremony'.

A detailed breakdown of the choir's repertoire, taken from the handwritten record entitled *Liturgy – Our Lady of Lourdes,* appears in Appendix III on page 192.

## At the organ

Philip Stephens is a former pupil of the Xaverian College, Brighton, and it was during his time there that he first learned to play the organ

**Servers pictured *c* 1971, with Father John Grant, seated centre. Back row: Mark Reade, Michael Johnson, Christopher Barber, Donald Carter, Philip Barber, Paul Turner, Dominic Turner, Paul Smith. Front row: Kevin Brown, Mark Brown, Master of Ceremonies Anthony Lee, Michael Gribbin, Clifton Mooney and Stephen Turner.** *Photo: Rosemary Reade.*

under the guidance of Mr Madle at St Bartholomew's church in Brighton. After graduating in law/history from London University, he went on to the Guildhall School of Music, where he obtained a teaching diploma. He subsequently joined a legal practice in Brighton. He was a lecturer for many years and still takes courses at the University of Brighton.

Philip's associations with Our Lady of Lourdes church go back to its beginnings. He played at the first Mass here in 1957 and thereafter on request. He was then resident organist at St John the Baptist, Kemp Town. It was not until one of the convent sisters who had regularly played at Benediction during the early years left that Philip was invited to be the regular organist. When the choir was formally established under Father Grant his place here was assured. He has given sterling service ever since, as the choir's former conductor, Anne Allinson, has placed on record:

'Throughout all the years, there would have been no music without Philip. He has been wonderfully faithful, long-suffering and brilliant. How many organists could produce Widor's Toccata out of a one-manual chamber organ with a straight, truncated pedal board? He is delightfully absent-minded at times and has to be prodded into action but always manages to rise to the occasion. His knowledge of plainsong notation and stress was very valuable in the early days when we sang so much Latin and the younger members had not had the advantage of Latin or plainsong in their education. Philip has on many occasions played at Arundel Cathedral and is additionally a competent pianist.'

## Steadfast servers

In the first few years of the new church and for a time before then, the server most regularly on the altar was perhaps Michael Thornton of Saltdean. He is the author of a number of biographical books, the subjects of which include Jessie Matthews and Anastasia.

Since Father Grant's time another resident of Saltdean, forty four year old Donald Carter, has been a constant server at the church. For twenty eight years up to 2000 he has helped to train many other servers in the necessary skills. Donald is a former pupil of Kingscliffe School, which is now part of Brighton College, and St Paul's, Haywards Heath.

Although no one can remotely claim to have served here for as many years as Donald, some young men such as William Davis, Nathan Day and Andrew Harvey have given long, sustained periods of service. On account of their studies and other commitments, they have had to discontinue serving on a regular basis but can on occasions still be seen on the altar, maintaining their link with the past.

## Cyril F F Butler 1972–1979

Father Cyril Butler served the parish of Our Lady of Lourdes for seven years, during which time, as his successor, Father McSheehey was to write in the *Rottingdean Church and Parish News* 'he endeared himself to so many, Catholics and non-Catholics alike, through his kindness, humanity and generosity'.

He was ordained in 1942 and worked in a number of parishes in the old Southwark diocese. When that was divided up in 1965 he found himself in the new diocese of Arundel and Brighton. Immediately prior to coming to Rottingdean, Father Cyril had been the parish priest of the Church of Our Lady, Queen of Heaven, in Frimley, Camberley, Surrey. It was there that he showed himself to be something of an entrepreneur.

He arrived there in 1957 and bought a house in Station Road. Three years earlier, a chapel had been created from a small barn in the grounds of the old Frimley Parsonage. When the owners of the land on which it stood decided to leave the district, the parish was obliged to buy the property. Thus, in 1959, Father Cyril found himself in possession of the Old Parsonage itself plus the chapel, a large kitchen garden and a field. The entire property cost less than £9,500.

With a view to the development of the field, he immediately sought planning permission for a housing estate – an initiative intended to pay off the expenses of the entire property and start a fund for a permanent church. Not until 1966, however, did he obtain permission to sell the land, known as The Cloisters, for development. With the revenue from this, he was able to proceed with plans for a church. Work began in May 1967 and at the end of November of that year, Frimley became a full parish. The new church, Our Lady, Queen of Heaven, was opened on the feast of St Peter and St Paul, 1969, much to the joy of the parishioners, who had been intolerably overcrowded in the old chapel during the two years in which building took place. The chapel was converted to a parish hall and in 1978 the old house was sold to the nuns of the Holy Family and became Frimley's first convent.

After fourteen years in that parish Father Cyril Butler moved to Rottingdean. The move was to some extent prompted by the fact that a large new hospital was being erected in Frimley and, as the bishop pointed out in a letter, 'there would be a considerable extra workload which would be best for a younger man.'

In a rare weekly parish notice sheet to have survived, dating from 20 August 1972, Father Cyril thanks the congregation for their generous response to the collection the previous Sunday for the Apostleship of the Sea which amounted to £33.84.

'However,' he noted, 'it seems it was a case of robbing Peter to pay Paul – the church collection went down to £66.41.'

With him from Frimley Father Butler had brought a set of Stations of the Cross, exquisitely painted and of quite exceptional value, which had belonged to the Empress Eugénie. Soon after his arrival in

**The sisters of St Martha's who 'help in every way possible in the life of the parish' pictured in the mid-1970s. Back row: Sisters Matthew, Angela, Margaret, Colette, Marie des Anges. Middle row: Sisters Louis Marie, St Edmund, Francis. Seated: Sisters Mary Pauline, Cécile and Jeanne d'Arc**

Rottingdean he gave them to the sisters at St Martha's Convent for their chapel, which had a set of similar size.

The convent that had given him the Stations for his new church, for which a parishioner had already carved a set, had in turn received them as a gift, probably when the contents of Eugénie's private chapel in Farnborough, Hampshire, were distributed. The Empress, who died in 1920, was the widow of Napoleon III who fled to England in 1870 after the disastrous Franco-Prussian war.

From a Dean's Visitation Form sent to Father Cyril in January 1975 it emerges that the housebound sick were visited monthly and enabled to have Holy Communion; that the last parish census had been made two years previously; and that the religious sisters 'help in every way possible in the life of the parish'. On the ecumenical front, the parish was a member of the Local Council of Churches and joint services were held four times a year. In regard to co-operation at social and welfare level 'everything possible is done.'

Under the heading 'pastoral projects or initiatives which had been tried with success in the parish' was 'joining with the Church of England in all village ceremonies, Rogation Sunday, Remembrance Day, joint Christmas Cards, helping to raise money for the recreation centre and homes for the elderly.' Yet young people were 'not at all involved in the life of the parish'. There was no play group nor any adult education projects. There was a parish pastoral council, although the only organisations and societies named were the Altar Society, the Church Cleaning Society and Mother Teresa's helpers.

Concerning parish missionary activities, the reply read 'a parish in Fiji'. In response to a question concerning any special financial problems there might be, was the wonderful Irish answer 'no, except the usual shortage of money.' During the years he was here, Father Cyril was popular with a fair number of his parishioners. More than one has described him as 'a man's man' while Molly Taylor called him 'everybody's friend.'

**Father Cyril at the White Horse Hotel after the wedding of Ian Lowington and Sheila De Rosa in 1977.**

He was a former Army man and an inveterate smoker who enjoyed a drink at the Rottingdean Club and other local venues. He also belonged to the local Lions. There were others, however, who felt that his life was too focused on the social side and that he did not take the needs of the children in the parish sufficiently into account. He clung to his authority in financial matters, to the extent that the parish council's finance committee no longer saw any reason for its existence and its members resigned *en bloc*. They included the chairman of the Parish Pastoral Council, a body evidently reinstated with some reluctance by Father Cyril in accordance with the new strictness on the part of the diocese in this connection.

The Dean's Visitation Report of December 1975 found that:

'Father Butler is very happy at Rottingdean and seems to be very much part of community life of the village. He has quite a rapport with non-Catholics, some of whom take their problems to him instead of to their own vicar. This is a welcome change from Father O'Brien's day when, I understand, Rottingdean was distinctly anti-Catholic.

'Yet Cyril keeps to himself as far as the Deanery priests are concerned and there is nothing that can be done about this. Obviously he is a man who believes in going it alone. It is hard to pin him down on anything and he is pretty hopeless at correspondence. So far I have not succeeded in getting a representative from the parish on the Deanery Pastoral Council but this matter is now under further consideration.

'The church is delightful and it is a shame that vandalism in the area makes it necessary to keep it closed during the winter for much of the day. Recently it was decorated to good effect by voluntary helpers from the parish.'

In the wider church context, the year 1975 was declared by Pope Paul VI to be a Holy Year. The Church normally sets aside a year every twenty five years for the renewal of Christian life, a renewal which involves certain spiritual exercises of an individual and community nature and various acts of penance and charity whereby reparation is made for sins, faith is strengthened and Christian love to fellow men rendered more effective.

The practice of Holy Year began in 1300 and carries on a custom described in the Old Testament. The Hebrew Jubilee Year was celebrated every fiftieth year. Men were invited to allow the land to rest so that it might recover its strength and fertility; to forgive debts which had accumulated against poor people and which the poor were unable to repay; and those who had unjustly accumulated riches at the expense of weaker members of the community were asked to restore their ill-gotten gains. Slaves were to be given their freedom. All of this was to be done in imitation of God's mercy which He had shown to Israel.

Father Cyril was charmingly vague and somewhat impractical in matters of business. In a letter to the bishop in response to a reminder to send in collections and accounts for 1975, he wrote 'my only excuse is that I am much happier with a brush or hammer in my hand than a pen.' Indeed, he did much of the decoration work on the church himself.

He suffered from cancer of the throat during his fifth year as parish priest, even though the tumour had initially been diagnosed as benign. The increasing severity of his affliction forced him, with reluctance, to relinquish his duties. The last mass he said in the church was on the feast of St Patrick 1979.

Bishop Cormac wrote this open letter of appreciation and thanks to the parish:

> I am writing to you first of all to express my grateful thanks to Father Cyril Butler for all the service he has given to the parish over these past years. Not only the parish, but also the diocese has much reason to be grateful to him for his devoted priestly work in different areas of the Lord's vineyard. As you know, he has suffered much and is at present still very ill. I need hardly ask you for your continued prayers for him that God will give him every consolation and blessing.
>
> I would also like to express my gratitude to you, the parishioners of Our Lady of Lourdes, for your concern for Father Butler and your devoted care of the parish. It is with confidence that I now commend Father John McSheehy to you as your parish priest. I am sure you will give him every support and help in his task of serving you in the parish.'

Father Cyril's health deteriorated rapidly during the next few months until finally, on 12 September, all his sufferings came to an end. His Requiem Mass in Our Lady of Lourdes church was attended by some fifty priests and many parishioners and friends, including the local clergy of other denominations. Bishop Cormac was the Principal Celebrant and was assisted by Father Toby Butler, Cyril's brother. Canon John O'Connor, parish priest of the Sacred Heart parish, Hove, preached. The congregation then walked in procession to St Margaret's churchyard for the burial service, which was conducted by Father Toby.

## Father John McSheehy 1979-1996

Under Father Butler's successor there was a period of sustained development and expansion, with the addition to the church of a new building – the parish room. John McSheehy was born in 1922 at Wimbledon and was educated at Ampleforth under the guidance of the Benedictines. One of his contemporaries there was the late Cardinal Basil Hume, Archbishop of Westminster.

After Ampleforth he attended the junior seminary at Mark Cross near Tunbridge Wells for a year and then, after a further six years at the diocesan seminary at Wonersh, he was ordained on 31 May 1947. His contemporary at Wonersh, John (now Canon) Stapleton, said of him:

> 'Our spiritual development as students for the priesthood was a rather hit-and-miss affair in those days for most of us. But one thing was central then, as it is now – the Mass. "It is the Mass that matters" we said. That conviction, for John, must have come as a natural progression from his schooldays under the Benedictines at Ampleforth.
> '31 May 1947. A boiling hot day it was. Sixteen of us were ordained in the seminary chapel by Archbishop Peter Amigo. None of us knew what the future would hold. The general expectation was of about twenty years as a curate before getting a parish of one's own. And indeed, John started that way, as curate at Plumstead'.

Father McSheehy vividly recalled the long fast before ordination. From midnight, and in very hot weather, he went without food or even a drink of water until the service was over well after midday. He stayed at the south east London parish of St Patrick, Plumstead, for three years. He was then sent to teach at St Peter's, Merrow, an independent grammar school run by the Guildford diocese and largely staffed by priests. Father McSheehy was given the job of teaching science, mainly, he admitted, because he started the headmaster's car by the judicious use of a halfpenny.

**Father John McSheehy**

After sixteen years at St Peter's he was posted in September 1966 to Langley Green, Crawley. This was his first job as parish priest, and he stayed there for three years, succeeding Father Gregory Williams, the founder priest of the parish. He then moved to Godalming, where he spent ten years before coming to Our Lady of Lourdes in 1979.

He arrived at a time when his qualities were badly needed and set about revitalising the spiritual and social life of the parish and also put financial matters on a sound footing. He saw to the renovation and redecoration of the presbytery and carried out a programme of repair and refurbishment of the church. In addition he found time to lead two highly successful pilgrimages, one to Lourdes and one to the Holy Land.

## The Rottingdean SVP

One of his first initiatives was to found a local group, traditionally called 'a conference', of the St Vincent de Paul Society. Started by a French law student, Frédéric Ozanam in 1843, this is an international Catholic organisation of lay people who seek to help by person-to-person involvement anyone who is suffering, whatever the cause. The society is open to all who wish to show practical love to their neighbour and the Rottingdean conference has consistently comprised six or seven active members, several of whom have been Anglicans. In 1981, the conference had twelve members and no fewer than a thousand visits were made. The primary work of the conference has always been visiting the sick, the housebound and the lonely of the parish in their homes, nursing homes or hospitals, but the caring has extended beyond that and beyond the parish and parishioners.

Over the years the conference has consistently made up to thirty or more visits per week, thanks to unfailing support from the parish priest

**An early SVP meeting in the presbytery. L to r: Ann Knox, Mary Jailie, Joyce Greenwood, Father McSheehy, John Remers, John Doyle, Joyce Brooks and Phyllis Chinn.**

and by planning activities at a weekly meeting. Through the immense generosity– and frequently direct participation – of parishioners, activities which people could otherwise not afford have become possible, such as children going to camp, sick people going to Lourdes and the elderly and disabled going on outings.

Members have joined with fellow-members of conferences in the area to initiate and run projects which serve all who are in acute need in Brighton and Hove. One such is the SVP Brighton Soup Run which serves hot soup every night of the year at Brighton seafront locations to anyone who needs it. Staffed by 150 volunteers who come mainly from religious groups of various denominations, the Soup Run served 16,000 in 1999. Another project is the SVP/Emmaus furniture scheme, which provides basic furnishings for people who, for whatever reason, cannot get assistance elsewhere.

Internationally, the conference helps two similar SVP conferences in areas of dire poverty in India by a regular exchange of prayers, correspondence and money. In these, and many other ways, the members and the volunteers they can call on can live the diocesan vision:

'To be Christ in our world, a community of love.
Partners in service, a source of hope for all,
Through God's power working in us.'

☆ ☆ ☆

The school buildings in 1987 with pupils on the bridge and, below, the buildings and bridge as they were in 1969.

# 9

# Our Lady of Lourdes School

THIS Aided Roman Catholic Primary School was opened in 1969 to cater for the local children who would otherwise have had to travel to Brighton to attend a Catholic school. At the time, a dozen or so were already making the journey to St John the Baptist School, Kemp Town, and it was initially accepted that the new school, if started, would administratively be an annexe of that establishment.

In the early days more children attended from Saltdean than any other outlying area. Woodingdean children had been accustomed to attending St John the Baptist and were not taken away from there until a year or two later when the Woodingdean priest ran a bus to and from Rottingdean for his parish's children. There were very few 'walking pupils' to begin with as property prices in Rottingdean were so high.

Currently Our Lady of Lourdes School has more than 200, mainly Catholic, children aged between four and eleven years, who come from Rottingdean, Saltdean, Telscombe Cliffs, Peacehaven, Woodingdean and Ovingdean. The original building has been modernised and extended to take seven classes, with twenty eight to thirty two pupils in each class. There is also a hall for assemblies, physical education and school lunches and two playgrounds. The school also has the use of a large playing field. The lending and reference library and the classrooms and teaching areas are now well equipped with books and other teaching resources but this was certainly not the case when the school first opened.

Had it not been for a telephone call made by a parishioner to the right person at the right time, Our Lady of Lourdes School would not have come into existence at all.

It was generally known when the 1964/65 school year began that it would be the last for St Martha's Convent School and that the premises would have to be sold. The nuns were naturally anxious for them to be sold to the diocese for educational purposes but were not in a position to promote their wishes in this respect publicly. Behind the scenes, however, they did put their case to Canon José, the Diocesan Director of Education. Father Patrick O'Brien was undoubtedly in favour of the school continuing but did not take any direct action, although pressure was placed upon him to by parents, particularly those with children who were going to schools in Brighton. In spite of reassurances, however, no tangible progress was being made.

Parishioner Ann Turner, two of whose children were making that journey, decided to write to the bishop. His reply was sent via Father O'Brien and was not relayed to her immediately. Mrs Turner therefore wrote again, enclosing a copy of her original letter.

This time the response was rapid and sent directly to her. The scheme would certainly be looked at. Father O'Brien frowned on this display of initiative – indeed, Mrs Turner was denounced from the pulpit as a 'self-appointed shop steward.' His annoyance was doubtless due in part to the exchange of correspondence having brought to light a delay on his part in submitting diocesan contributions.

## A vital telephone call

Still nothing was done. More meetings were called and there was strong support among local parents for action to be taken while there was still time. Losing patience, Mrs Turner telephoned Canon José. He was surprised that she was unaware that the premises were to be put up for sale by auction – and inevitably redevelopment. The letter to the nuns advising them of the diocese's intention to withdraw from its proposed purchase was on his desk and due to be sent out the next day. Because of Mrs Turner's call, he agreed to come down and see the schoolrooms for himself and chair a meeting at the convent at which all points of view could be heard.

The meeting was a great success from the parents' point of view. Mrs Turner showed Canon José round the annexe, where he could see for himself that the block of five ready-made classrooms was simply waiting to be re-opened. He agreed that the diocese should step in and take over the complex, including the property known as Pax, which had served the five to eighteen year olds at St Martha's. This house was sold to Jack and Collette Flanagan who were then living in Saltdean. Father Grant, who had succeeed Father O'Brien, appointed Mrs Flanagan as head teacher of the new school and Mrs Colette Wholey as assistant head.

For a couple of months in the spring of 1969 the two members of staff worked hard, ordering furniture, books and equipment and all necessities for a grand opening. However, there was a delay in the building works and a letter of apology had to go out to parents telling them that the opening was delayed. Finally all was in readiness and the school received its first pupils on 5 May 1969 – not a normal start date for a school but this did not really matter to Collette or her deputy.

'It turned out to be a lovely sunny day, and so with registers and pens at the ready we sat waiting for the arrival of hordes of parents and children,' she said. 'At the end of the day we had enrolled eighteen'.

## The first eighteen

| No. | Surname | Christian Name | Where from |
|---|---|---|---|
| 1 | Barratt | Mark Anthony | Telscombe Cliffs |
| 2 | Cresci | Andrea Louise | Woodingdean |
| 3 | Dare | Bridget Anne | Woodingdean |
| 4 | Murphy | Paul Francis | Saltdean |
| 5 | Spalding | Caroline Mary | Saltdean |
| 6 | Stewart | Karl | Saltdean |
| 7 | Taylor | Lisa Clare | Saltdean |
| 8 | Turner | Susan Ann | Rottingdean |
| 9 | Vincent | Corinne Huguette Jocelyne | Saltdean |
| 10 | Boyce | Angela Mary | Rottingdean |
| 11 | Bryce | Patricia Frances | Saltdean |
| 12 | Cresci | Paul Charles | Woodingdean |
| 13 | D'Mello | Felicity Irene Maria | Saltdean |
| 14 | Johnson | Wendy Ann | Saltdean |
| 15 | Mooney | Grainne | Woodingdean |
| 16 | Stewart | Kathleen | Saltdean |
| 17 | Tiernan | Kevin Michael | Woodingdean |
| 18 | Turner | Stephen | John Rottingdean |

**Some of the school's first pupils in the playground.**

With the buildings having a capacity for four classes of thirty each, 120 in all, the initial intake seemed, and was, small. No doubt it was due to the unusual time of year for a new term to begin. There were many interruptions in the first two terms. The school was closed for the local elections on 8 May, for Ascension Day on 15 May and then on 23 May for half term. When it re-opened on 2 June, Mrs Wholey was off for the day with food poisoning. It then closed on 5 and 6 June for Corpus Christi.

The first meeting of the school managers was on 20 June and was described by Mrs Flanagan as 'friendly and very helpful'. Canon José joined in to discuss the financial position and the managers looked over the school and were impressed with what had been accomplished in such a short time.

## The official opening

The school's official opening was scheduled for 26 June and the builders endeavoured to complete the decoration of the extension in time for it, working right up to midnight on 24 June. Bishop David

**Smiles for a press photographer from Bishop David Cashman and the children who 'behaved perfectly' at the opening ceremony.**

Cashman blessed and officially opened the school on the appointed day. His attack on humanists trying to take religious education out of the schools in this country was widely reported in the local and national press. Among the distinguished visitors at the ceremony was Brighton's Director of Education, the headmasters of neighbouring Christian schools, the head of the C of E school, and the Reverend Ivor Walters, vicar of Rottingdean. Owing to an oversight they did not sign the Visitors' Book.

The parents met a couple of weeks later to discuss the school uniform and agreed the colours would be scarlet and grey. Today pupils wear a light blue and white striped tie with a white shirt, grey jumper, and grey skirt or trousers.

On 24 July the school closed for the summer holidays after an exacting and busy first term. 'We are very happy with our lovely children and the parents are very happy with their school,' wrote Mrs Flanagan in the school log.

The first full school year of 1969/70 began in September with an increase in numbers to thirty seven. An additional part-time teacher was immediately requested, at first unsuccessfully.

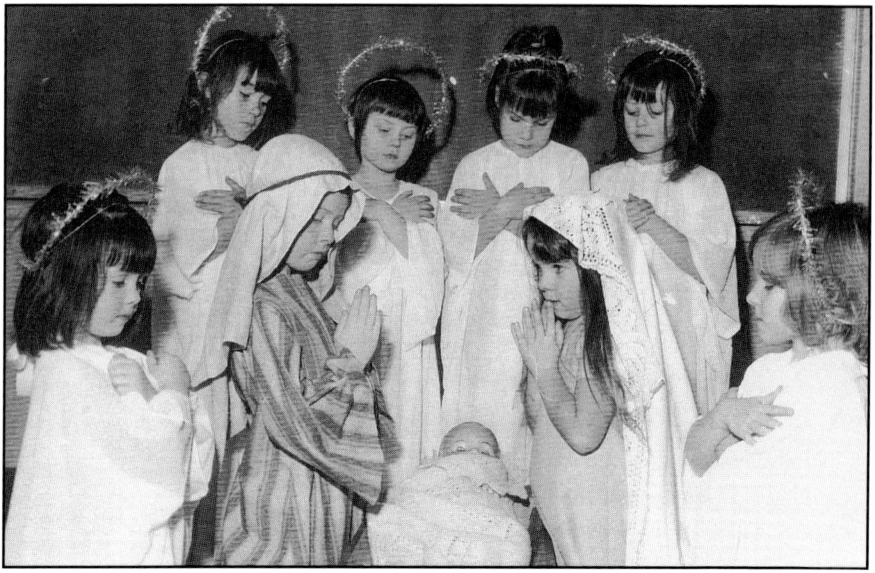

**The first Nativity play at the school in December 1969.**

*Photo: Evening Argus*

A nursery class was opened in January to cater for fourteen children who were admitted. In mid-April the arrival of six new pupils raised the total to fifty seven. Mrs Murphy was the teacher. Nursery assistant Ann Turner joined the staff and remained until July, when she went as a mature student to the College of Education. She was replaced in the autumn by Mrs Bryce. Ann Turner did return later, leaving again at Christmas 1973, after which time she became a supply teacher.

## Highlights from the school log

Towards the end of March parents successfully approached Canon José with the request that Our Lady of Lourdes be made a five to eight year old school as soon as possible. A deputation met the Director of Education, Mr K Antcliffe, to reinforce this request. He responded sympathetically, and the parents' efforts won the approval of the Chapter Authorities. 'The whole thing', records the school log, 'was accomplished in a most dignified and orderly manner.'

Miss Ellis from the Education Office visited the school to advise on how to erect and use the PE apparatus but this did not prevent young Alison Gibbs breaking her arm while exercising on it the following summer.

In early June 1970, ten children made their first Holy Communion and afterwards there was a tea party for them. Midway through the month the school's first Open Evening was held and it featured a display of the children's work. On 18 June the school was open to the public as part of Brighton's Education Centenary celebrations. It was inundated with visitors all day and local councillors came in spite of the General Election. The children behaved extremely well and normal teaching went on throughout the day.

In September it re-opened with fifty eight on the roll and a further nine were admitted after the Easter holidays. Quite a ceremony was made of Father Grant's blessing of the school's new tapestry which had been presented by Mrs Murphy, whose daughter Katharine was at the school. At the end of the month, Mr Finnie, the headmaster of Fitzherbert School, Woodingdean, which was to be re-organised and form a Middle School into which Our Lady of Lourdes children would be fed, spent the morning at the school to see the childrens' work. 'This bodes well', Mrs Flanagan wrote in the log, 'for the future education of our children.'

The Christmas activities and nativity play were performed to a more than full house at the village hall. Nearly £30 was collected at the door, half of which was sent to the *Argus* appeal for Brighton's needy.

On 17 January 1972, Mrs Bayliss, one of the managers, visited the school to discuss a proposed extension, namely a kitchen, hall, and other offices. A managers' meeting was held early the following month and Canon José, the diocesan representative, agreed to approach the Brighton Education Authority on the matter.

Drama came towards the end of March with the evacuation of the school due to a bomb scare. Mrs Flanagan was advised that there was little danger in returning to the building. However, in view of the fact that this was a Catholic school, she decided to take no risks and kept the children and staff on the top field until the end of the school session.

After the bomb scare came a break-in. The thief or thieves had a total haul of 10½p but damaged some windows, doors and cupboards.

A more pleasant occasion was the farewell ceremony for Father Grant, who was leaving to take up a post at Arundel. The children presented him with an oil painting in appreciation of all he had done for the school.

The boys' football team had its first fixture – against the boys of St John the Baptist – and lost 8-7. In an incident quite unconnected with the match, young Louise Allen fell and broke her arm.

The end of July saw the departure of Mrs Murphy, who was moving to the Liverpool area. The children gave a farewell concert and presented her with an oil painting of the village pond.

In the autumn term the number on the roll passed the 100 mark for the first time and permission was given for Mrs Wholey to be appointed deputy head, although strictly the numbers did not qualify for such a post. In November, there was a full day's holiday from school to celebrate the Royal Silver Wedding and the children wrote letters of greeting to the Queen and the Duke of Edinburgh.

The Christmas entertainment provided by the school made headlines in the *Brighton and Hove Gazette* on 16 December 1972:

**ROTTINGDEAN'S LITTLE ANGELS ENTERTAIN**

> One hundred and one little angels, all children of Our Lady of Lourdes School, Rottingdean, delighted parents and friends on Sunday with a programme of entertainment for Christmas. Because the school has no hall large enough to take all those who wanted to see the show, the Headmaster of Longhill School, Mr R Morley, put the hall and changing rooms at the disposal of the infant school. While the audience of 400 were enchanted by the school band (average age four and half), conducted by Mrs Pauline Keenan, the French Episode, enacted by a class of eight year olds, was particularly impressive and a tribute to their teacher, Mrs J Packer.
>
> Guest of honour this year was Mrs D V Edney, mother of an eight year old handicapped boy at the school. She was chosen to represent all the parents who, as the school's headmistress Mrs Collette Flanagan stressed, played such an active part in creating the school's happy atmosphere. Mrs Edney was presented with a basket of flowers by Helen Ashdown, aged four, and eight year old Angela Boyle made a similar presentation to Mrs Flanagan. Other notable items enjoyed by the appreciative audience were *Dick Whittington,* produced by

Mrs Valerie Weston, and a production starring the older children, directed by Mrs Colette Wholey. Mrs Sue Fletcher, mother of two girls at the school, was responsible for make-up, helped by students at Longhill.

On 19 February 1973 it was decided, without opposition, at a meeting in Brighton's Council Chamber, to publish the Public Notices for Catholic Schools Re-organisation which would incorporate a three-form entry Middle School at Fitzherbert School. The following month, the children to be transferrred were taken with their parents, by Mrs Flanagan and Mrs Wholey, to see their new school and be introduced to their teachers. When term began, the bus carrying pupils from Bannings Vale, Saltdean, to Woodingdean ran half-empty, so a lot of the infants were allowed to use it free of charge and were dropped off in Rottingdean en route.

When parents Roy and Pauline Butler returned to the parish in 1973/74 they became involved, like so many others, in Parent-Teacher Association fundraising for the school hall and a kitchen. Meals were then being served in the corridor and Pauline helped Joan Moore with them when necessary. On one occasion Roy, who was a governor of the school from 1975 to 1979, had to borrow a Baby Burco to boil all the rice needed on a Curry Evening. Other families involved in fundraising included the Pierces, the Knoxs and the Mills, all from Saltdean. Their target was to raise the diocese's fifteen per cent share of the cost of a new hall, the balance coming from the council.

**Colette Wholey holds up a giant cheque for £12,600 – the sum raised by the PTA for the hall.**

On 11 February 1974, the feast of Our Lady of Lourdes, Holy Mass was celebrated in school for the first time.

On the staffing front, Mrs Huguette Vincent succeeded assistant

**The staff in 1979 after the classes had been re-named. L to r: Mrs Wholey, Mrs Flanagan, Mrs Taylor, Mrs Muir, Mrs Nowacki, Mrs Vincent and Mrs Sweeney.**

teacher Mrs Corrigan, who was leaving due to pregnancy, although she continued to work part-time for a while and Mrs Brenda Taylor took over as welfare assistant from Mrs Stacey, who left the school in June after five and half years of dedicated service to take up a full-time post at the University School. Later in the month there was temporarily no caretaker, as a result of injury, and Mrs Flanagan endeavoured to clean the school herself.

With the transfer of twenty seven pupils to Woodingdean at the end of the school year, numbers on the roll were reduced to seventy eight.

On 30 June 1975 building work started for the new extension and went on throughout the holidays. Thirty new children were admitted, plus two the next day, and the school started the new term under very great difficulties as workman were still putting the finishing touches to the extension. However, the log states, the staff 'came up to their usual standards and performed small miracles.'

At the end of February 1976, Miss R A Shepperd was named as the replacement for Mrs Thomas who was due to leave at the end of term.

When the autumn term began, thirty nine children were admitted over a period of three weeks. Mrs Flanagan had decided to stagger the intake to make the change from home to school easier. With fewer being admitted each week, mothers could remain with their children until they settled in and made friends.

The classes were renamed and the teachers were allocated as follows:

Class A, the reception class, Miss Shepperd
Class B, five to six years, Miss Walters
Class C, six to seven years, Mrs Vincent
Class D seven to eight years, Mrs Wholey.

Miss Shepperd married and became Mrs Weir. She was later replaced by Mrs Alcock and Mrs Sweeney subsequently took over from Miss Walters.

When school re-opened after half-term, the six-monthly inspection of the new buildings took place and a large number of faults were found and listed for correction. The builders failed to appear for many weeks. and it was learned in January that the firm was going into liquidation but that it would complete the school's work.

To mark the Queen's Silver Jubilee, prizes were offered to the children at both Our Lady of Lourdes and the C of E primary school for poems, paintings and essays on the village and its preservation.

At the start of the autumn term 1977 the number on the school roll reached 115. The following May, Mass was offered at school twice by Father Leonard Turner, on Ascension Day and on the feast of Corpus Christi. In June, Moira Muir was appointed to the permanent staff.

When school re-opened in the autumn of 1978, seventeen new children were admitted, the first group of a staggered intake of thirty eight which brought the roll up to 138. The school had a staff of four full-time teachers and one part-time teacher at this time. Children were drawn from Woodingdean and Peacehaven parishes as well as from Rottingdean, Ovingdean and Saltdean. Father Mulvey from Woodingdean sold his car and bought a minibus to transport his parish's children to school each day, and continued to do so until the numbers qualified for the hiring of a bus from Woodingdean.

**The group of nineteen children who made their First Communion on the school's tenth anniversary.** *Photo: Arthur Wain*

**Mrs Vincent with her pupils in 1979.**

## Celebrating the first decade

The tenth anniversary of the opening of Our Lady of Lourdes School was celebrated on 17 May 1979. Canon Bernard José, Canon John Grant who had conducted the opening ceremony, Father Edmund Geoghegan and Father Leonard Turner concelebrated the Mass. The parish priest, Father Cyril Butler, was at this time too ill to attend. The Sisters from St Martha's Convent were present, as were the foundation pupils, who were then students at Cardinal Newman School.

A group of nineteen children made their first Holy Communion and all the pupils sang the Mass, which had been composed for them by Mrs Maggie Larkin, one of the parents. They read the lessons, and carried the offertory gifts in procession. Afterwards, the governors, their guests, priests, teachers and the other members of staff joined the children at a sumptuous lunch prepared by the school cook, Mrs Coomber, and her staff.

No fewer than thirty four new children were admitted in September 1979 and three more in the following January. This again brought the number of pupils on the roll to 138. Of this number, some 20 per cent were non-Catholic. Despite the expansion of the building, a number of children had to be turned away and the disappointed parents included many non-Catholics.

At Christmas, a mime was produced at the altar in the church to a packed congregation and on the patronal feast on 11 February a school Mass, composed for the occasion by Maggie Larkin and dedicated to them, was sung by the pupils.

At the end of April 1980, the school was covered in soot. There had been a fire in the adult cloakrooms over the weekend which had burnt itself out, but there was evidence of it everywhere.

At the Interschool Football Cup Final in mid-June the school beat St Joseph's but then lost to Saint John the Baptist, Kemp Town.

In October 1980 Collette Flanagan tendered her resignation as head teacher, to take effect from the following 30 April. The *Rottingdean Church and Parish News* paid its tribute to her with these words:

> 'There was a famous occasion some years ago when Mrs Collette Flanagan stood up at a meeting on schools and proclaimed 'I am Our Lady of Lourdes.' The meeting dissolved into uncontrollable mirth but understood in the right way, there is a great deal of truth in that statement.

'For over eleven years now, the names of Our Lady of Lourdes School and Mrs Flanagan have become synonymous. As the school's first headmistress she started with eighteen children and has formed and guided it, with loving care and dedication, until today it is bursting at the seams and such is its reputation that many who are not members of our Church are seeking admission for their children. Mrs Flanagan now feels, reluctantly, that after a lifetime spent in Catholic schools, the time has come to make way for a younger person and to be able to enjoy a little leisure after a long life of selfless devotion. It is with great regret that the governors have accepted her resignation, to take effect from the end of the Spring Term 1981, but they fully understand her reasons. . .'

**Collette Flanagan with the scroll which accompanied the Papal Cross, *Pro Ecclesia et Pontifice,* she was awarded for services to Catholic education.**
*Photo: John Hughes*

Mrs Flanagan's last day as head teacher at the school was 10 April 1981. She wrote in the log:

'I am deeply touched by the love and kindness shown to me by everyone. I thank Almighty God and Our Lady of Lourdes for giving me the health and strength to undertake the very responsible and privileged task of educating our little ones. May they keep my successor ever in their care and my good wishes and prayers are with you, Mr Beardow. . . '

## A change at the helm 1981-1989

Reginald Beardow's introduction to Rottingdean was the annual parish meeting on 22 October 1980. From it he learned that the school was a great help in binding the parish together and that it enjoyed a good relationship with the clergy in Rottingdean and Saltdean.

New admissions in September 1981 were thirty one, bringing the total children to 132. The Department of Education and Science gave formal approval for the extension of a sub-standard classroom and the work was done that autumn by Saltdean builder, Mr M Challoner of Rodmell Avenue. When inspected six months later 'no defects needing remedy' were found.

In February 1982, a fire engine and crew from Roedean came to the playground to demonstrate firefighting equipment to the children. In June, there was a visit after school by a party of twenty four children and their teachers from St Mary's RC Primary School, Chesterfield, Derbyshire. They were visiting Rottingdean under the family association of parishioners Brian and Ann Turner and were allowed to use the hall and fields for their tea-time break following a tour of the village and celebration of Holy Mass at Our Lady of Lourdes church.

On 15 July, the whole school went on an outing together for the first time. Two double-decker buses took them, with teachers and a group of parent helpers, to Drusillas Zoo Park at Alfriston.

The logbook ends on 3 September 1982, the day after the school re-opened for the autumn term. The last entry was: 'Wasp nest discovered over main entrance doors.' No new logbook was started for three years.

Although the school was operating successfully and at full capacity, curtailments and economies caused by the 1984 education budget cuts had resulted in worsening pupil/teacher ratios. In September 1985, thirty four new pupils were admitted. Of these, fourteen were to be full-time, nine were to come in Monday to Wednesday and eleven on Mondays, Thursdays and Fridays. By half term all were full-time.

Our Lady of Lourdes School was not the only one bursting at the seams at this time. A new boy, a non-Catholic, was admitted in January because the village school was full. It was only because Class 4, for which he was eligible, had twenty seven children instead of the thirty it was intended to accommodate that he could be accepted.

Two new part-timers joined the staff and the teaching structure now stood at: Acting head, until 31 August 1986, Mrs Colette Wholey; deputy head and Class 4, Mrs S Sweeney; Class 3, Miss T Wilding; Class 2, Mrs M Muir; Reception Class, Mrs S Cullen.

The severe weather conditions affecting the whole locality caused a disruption to the school routine on 7 February 1986. There had been overnight snow and the roads were so bad that the school buses were all cancelled. Mrs Wholey went into school early and found the caretaker was there and the cook. Parents were advised that, although the school

**The staff with their new head teacher. Standing: Mrs Taylor and Mrs Muir. Seated, l to r: Mrs Sally Sweeney, who retired in 1999 after 27 years' service, Mr Beardow, Mrs Wholey and Mrs Vincent.**

was open, it would not be wise for children from any distance to come in. In the event, nine children and three teachers turned up – and they all made a snowman. The teachers were sent home after lunch as they had to walk over icy roads.

Colette Wholey deputised for Reg Beardow when he went on a year's sabbatical to study at London University, where he was to gain a Diploma in Education. On his return he was dismayed to find gallons of water flowing out of the overflow at the rear of the school. The cause was a broken ballcock on the main cold water tank.

At about this time Brighton Education Authority decided to revert to two-tier education and make Our Lady of Lourdes a primary school for five to eleven year olds. To this end the buildings needed to be extended and the school was moved to the School at Woodingdean while the work was done. Plans for the extension were greeted with strong objections from Rottingdean Preservation Society but planning permission was granted in 1987. Building work started the following January and was due to finish in September 1989 – the twentieth anniversary of the school.

The new building was to cost some £530,000 of which the governors and Catholic parishioners in the area served by the school would have to find about £80,000. On this occasion the diocese agreed to fund the governors' contributions, along with those of the governors of St John the Baptist's and St Joseph's schools, from the proceeds of the sale of Fitzherbert School. This building was eventually demolished and a Nuffield Hospital now occupies its site.

## Progress and achievements since 1989

In September 1989, Brian Sheed, the head at the time of writing, was appointed to replace Reg Beardow, who had accepted a post in Australia. At his induction during the 10.15am Mass on 15 October, the members of the congregation were asked to commit themselves by a solemn promise to support the new head by prayers and active encouragement. The keys were then handed over to him by the parish priest and everyone was invited to look round the school, which had re-opened the previous month after a year of re-building work. And for the new school there was a new logo. The design of an English rose in the centre of a Celtic cross, the whole bordered by a circle of rosary beads, was the winning entry in a competition.

Yet during the summer some felt the refurbishment had not gone far enough. Concern was expressed about the lack of playing fields and the size of the play area. Junior members of staff, who visited the school in July, thought that the classrooms were small, that there was too little cloakroom space and that toilet facilities for junior children were minimal. The school itself looked pleasant but its grounds had not been landscaped.

The buildings did provide much improved facilities although when the school 'came home' from its sojourn at Woodingdean there was no caretaker, no cleaners and it was two kitchen staff short. There was, however, a fairly full complement of staff consisting of:

| | | | |
|---|---|---|---|
| Reception | Mrs M Waddington | Year Four | Mrs G Collings |
| Year One | Mrs S Cullen | Year Five | Mrs C Wholey |
| Year Two | Mrs B Milham | Year Six | Mr D Mitchell |
| Year Three | Mrs S Sweeney | | Mrs M Oxley (part-time) |

The doors were re-opened on 5 September 1989 with 206 children on the roll, thirty one of whom were new entrants in the Reception Class. Class sizes varied from thirty three in Year 1 to twenty six in Year 5. Then it was down to work, enlivened by a certain amount of play, and plays, according to some of the entries in the resumed school log.

On 18 November the Kinetic Theatre Company presented a science-based play about the environment. The company was back again in March 1992 with more science drama, this time entitled *What a Gas.* In May that year the school had a joint music and singing session with Rottingdean C of E Primary School.

As well as day excursions, such as the trip to London for 100 children in December 1991 organised by the PTA and Year 6's visit to Portsmouth to see HMS *Victory* and other famous ships, there were residential visits lasting up to a week. In June 1992, Year 5 children spent five days on the Isle of Wight – a trip repeated in 1994 – and Year Six went to Canute House at Poole in Dorset. In 1993 Year Five and Year Six went together for a week at Gaveston Hall, near Horsham

The school's first computer was installed in 1992 – in the office to be used for finance and administration. A few more years would pass before there were PCs for pupils to use. A three-day inspection in December that year resulted in a most complimentary report on the school. The excellent quality of the relationships between staff and pupils and between the pupils themselves was especially commended. There was a slight drop in numbers to 200 in the autumn of 1993 and at the end of the school year, Colette Wholey, one of the original staff members, retired after twenty five years service. She was succeeded by Mrs Joan Lenham, then deputy head of St Mary Magdalen RC School, Brighton.

## Silver jubilee celebrations

The school celebrated its silver jubilee in May 1994. A marquee was hired, food and entertainment provided, guests arrived – and it poured with rain the whole time. In spite of the weather more than 400 people had a thoroughly enjoyable evening, thanks principally to the indefatigable PTA which did most of the organising. Mrs Collette Flanagan, the first head teacher, recalled the early years of Catholic education in Rottingdean and looked to the future with confidence.

'The future of Our Lady of Lourdes School looks secure,' she said. 'It

**The school's first pupil, Mark Barratt, unveils the Silver Jubilee plaque.**

has a very good name for the excellence of the education it provides and for the behaviour of the pupils. May I take this opportunity to congratulate all concerned who have worked so hard to build on the foundation that Mrs Wholey and I optimistically laid with great love in 1969 with the help of our good secretaries, Mrs Joyce Stacey and Mrs Brenda Taylor. May the school go from strength to strength and may Almighty God pour his blessings on the children and staff who follow in the years ahead.'

The silver jubilee is marked for posterity by a plaque in the school hall. It was unveiled by Mark Barratt, Bob Copper's grandson and the first of the eighteen pupils enrolled by Mrs Flanagan and Mrs Wholey on 5 May 1969.

## Academic achievements

The last entry in the log refers to the closing of the school for the summer holidays in 1994. A new data-based system of recording information was introduced in the new school year.

In 1997/98 the school came third overall in the National Curriculum SATS test league table. Eighty seven per cent of seven year olds achieved

**The whole school pictured on the playground in 1998.**
*Photo: Evening Argus.*

at least the Government-set standards in English, eighty one per cent in maths, and eighty seven per cent in science. Head teacher Brian Sheed attributed Rottingdean's good results to the support of parents and the dedication of the teachers. 'There is a very active PTA now raising up to £6,000 a year and the parents are giving their children essential encouragement in and out of lessons,' he said. 'And our older children are expected to do five hours homework a week – a lot more than in most primaries'.

The proportion of Catholic pupils at the school was by then ninety per cent. Religious education was a core subject and took up twice the amount of time it did in non-denominational schools.

Academic success was achieved again in 1998/99 when the school came first out of the forty primary schools in Brighton and Hove in the latest assessment based on standards in English, maths and science.

November 2000 marked the end of another chapter in the school's story as Brian Sheed announced his intention of resigning at Easter to take up a peripatetic role within the diocese.

☆ ☆ ☆

# 11

# Landmarks of the Eighties

## A local war hero

The death occurred at his home in France in 1981 of a prominent Catholic with Rottingdean associations, Count Anne-Pierre d'Harcourt, the second husband of Laurian Jones, daughter of Enid Bagnold and Sir Roderick Jones. Her parents had initially opposed Laurian's planned marriage to Pierre because he had been married already and belonged to a family so Catholic that civil divorce was not recognised. However, the divorce did ultimately take place and the couple married on 11 July 1955. During the 1960s, they lived in The Elms, given to Laurian by her mother, and here they brought up their children, Thierry and Harriet. Pierre, a journalist, contributed travel articles to the *Observer.*

Few knew of his wartime exploits which he recounted in *The Real Enemy,* the book in which he gives a first-hand account of life – if it can be called life – as a prisoner of the Third Reich.

He joined the Resistance forces in his native France but was betrayed and fell into the hands of the Gestapo. When trying to escape he was shot four times, but miraculously survived to endure two and a half years of solitary confinement in Fresnes, the impregnable redoubt in Paris. From there he was moved to a small 'reprisal camp' at Neue Bremm near Saarbrücken where prisoners were systematically ill treated so they would need minimum supervision at their final destination – a concentration camp.

Pierre was sent to Buchenwald, where he remained under atrocious conditions until the end of the war. It was only later that he learned that he had, in fact, been sentenced to death when in Fresnes yet fate somehow decreed otherwise. Buchenwald was virtually a death sentence in itself – for most prisoners it simply meant that they were not recorded as formally executed by the Reich.

Throughout his imprisonment, it was his faith which sustained him. The rosary became paramount, all the more so since one had been given to him as an act of kindness by his warder in Fresnes, a corporal in the German army. It was only when he thanked God for his captivity and kissed his chains that Pierre found the peace and courage to continue.

**Count Pierre d'Harcourt in the garden room of North End House in the early 1960s.**

After the war, it was a long time before he could adjust to normal life. When his sister married in his parish church, he felt unable to go inside and later he felt unequal to joining the reception. The way of the normal world was to him an insult and mockery to those who had lived and died in Buchenwald. Pierre, yearning to make up to himself the youth he had lost, wanted to forget he was old and weak, so he married a girl of seventeen, 'really only because she was young and healthy and full of life. Of course, there was no happiness to it and inevitably it failed.'

Despite the severe injuries to his legs sustained during the war, Pierre was a great walker and he and Laurian would go for long strolls along the Undercliff. Charming yet reserved, he was known only to a few villagers who remembered him as an outwardly ordinary man and were astonished to learn what he had gone through.

The d'Harcourts left The Elms in 1970 to settle in France.

## Preparing for the Pope's visit

Ninety five Rottingdean parishioners were among the 1,400 from all over the Brighton Deanery who attended Mass at the Dome, Brighton, on 4 February 1982 and heard Bishop Cormac stress the need for real spiritual preparation for the forthcoming visit of the Pope. 'This is vital,' he said, 'if the visit is to be more than a mere fiesta and is to have a lasting effect on our commitment to the Gospel message'. Mass was concelebrated by the bishop with all the priests of the Deanery. The organ was played by our organist, Philip Stephens; the choir was provided by Cardinal Newman School; and Ann Knox represented Rottingdean in the offertory procession.

Fifty-one tickets were allotted to the parish for the Papal Mass at Wembley on 29 May, and one or two were available to members of other churches who wished to join Our Lady of Lourdes on that occasion.

On 11 February, as every year, the feast of Our Lady of Lourdes and Patronal Feast, was celebrated. The 10am Mass that day was attended by a large number of parishioners and the children from the school led the singing of the special Mass, written for them by Mrs Maggie Larkin.

## Silver Jubilee year

Bishop Cormac celebrated the 10.15 Mass at Our Lady of Lourdes on 13 June, the silver jubilee of the opening of the church. There he met Robert and Leslie Moppett, the brothers who, with their three usual skilled craftsman, had built it. After the service there was a reception for parishioners to meet the bishop at the Whiteway Centre, where a buffet was provided by members of the Guild of St Martha and helpers.

**Father McSheehy, Robert and Leslie Moppett and Bishop Cormac.** *Photo: Brighton and Hove Herald.*

**The Rottingdean pilgrims at Lourdes. See facing page 157 for the names.**

## Lourdes Pilgrimage of Thanksgiving

The parish also marked its silver jubilee with a pilgrimage to the shrine of Our Lady in Lourdes organised by the late Yvonne Hope, a former parishioner whose last years were spent in Eastbourne. Her own visits to Lourdes had been made independently, the first of them in 1965. It was then that she first met a cured case in the person of Mme Winifred A Feely and learned from her lectures at the Medical Bureau about her miracle:

> 'I had cancer between the heart and the pulmonary artery which had grown to such proportions that all hope of treatment was abandoned. I had had seven major operations, all in vain; I had been on my back for many years. All my doctors were against my coming to Lourdes. But I wanted to come to ask for the grace to bear my suffering and perhaps to help somebody else. I had also a curvature of the spine, and a very bad ulcer. I was taken to the baths and plunged into the icy water. It was unbearable and I did not want to go again. I prayed to Our Lady to reveal to me something I could do of value before I died. The fourth day after the bath I had the worst night of suffering I could ever remember. I was wheeled to the Grotto, and as I lay there praying I heard a voice, telling me to go and take another bath. I was wheeled once more to the baths and plunged into the water. I walked from the baths on my own feet, completely cured'

Mme Feely showed X-rays of her chest before and after the cure. There was no trace of illness. For the thirty four years since the miracle she had been a helper at the Medical Bureau and for six months each year used to lecture on Lourdes in the United States.

Specialists from all parts of the world and of all faiths, or of no faith, attended the inquiries at the Medical Bureau. The religious aspect did not enter into their work at all – they were only required to furnish proofs of their medical qualifications. Each inquiry was discussed

**Front row, Nicola and Benedict Stanberry and Mrs Heather Stanberry. Second row, seated: Pat and Margaret Fallon, Phyllis Chinn, Pamela Hayward, Sister Matthew, Father McSheehy, Sister Mary Pauline, Kay and Ralph Pacitti, Moira Casey. Third row: Joe and Margaret Kerrigan, Gladys Gilles, Ray Hayward, Margaret Potier, Ivy and Eddie McAuley, Teresa Caillard, Margaret Worte, Edith Stanberry, Jean Caillard, Jean and Dusty Miller, Winifred Goulding. Fourth row: Beryl Derrington, Arthur Stanberry, Elizabeth Barnes, Bill and Jean Cox, Chris Caillard, Ann Knox, Michael Stanberry. Back row: Edith McSheehy, Mary and Ken Hardingham, Yvonne Hope, John Knox.**

without any religious bias, and if any single factual detail of an inquiry was missing such as radiographs or, in the case of a cancer cure which had received X-ray treatment, medical evidence that the treatment had been a total failure, that inquiry would not be proceeded with.

In 1980, returning from her last visit before the Silver Jubilee year, Yvonne could see from her train window the distant Basilica, already filling with pilgrims for the first Mass. As she gazed at the scene in the early morning sunlight, she sensed a strong message being conveyed to her: 'Bring people from your parish to this place.' And so it happened.

She approached Father McSheehy shortly after her return with her proposal for the pilgrimage. He was somewhat surprised. For some time he had been wondering what event could possibly be organised to mark the church's jubilee. Here, of course, was the answer.

He gave a talk on Lourdes, illustrated with coloured slides, to the Guild of St Martha on 23 June 1982 and four days later those planning to go on the pilgrimage met to finalise arrangements. He decided to extend an invitation to join the group to the parish of St Joan of Arc, Farnham, with which he had close associations. The combined party of forty two flew out on 30 July 1982 and returned on 6 August.

Mme Feely celebrated her eighty fifth birthday in Lourdes on 31 July and Yvonne Hope visited her in her small office in the Medical Bureau to wish her a happy day. On the following Wednesday, the group from Rottingdean attended one of her lectures and were told of a recent cure at the baths. A young Italian soldier whose hip bone had completely disintegrated because of a serious bone disease had arrived encased in plaster. He was unable to move and was lowered into the baths just as he was. When he returned to the military hospital in Italy, the cast was removed, his hip was again X-rayed and the plate showed a perfect, re-formed hip bone. The young soldier was soon on his feet again, completely healthy.

## With ACROSS to Lourdes

These days, some visits to Lourdes are made through the ACROSS organisation to which Ann Knox has given many years of service. The ACROSS Trust, a registered charity which has been operating more than twenty five years, conveys groups of patients in jumbo-sized ambulances known as Jumbulances to Lourdes, where it has an establishment named L'Astazou Across. This is a complex of three houses, each one essentially a self-contained home with doctors and nurses in attendance.

A typical ACROSS group consists of a group leader who is responsible for finding enough patients to fill a Jumbulance and the necessary attendant carers to look after them on the journey and during their week's stay at L'Astazou. The leader is also responsible for financing the trip, but more often than not it is underwritten by a parish or a charitable organisation.

A fully loaded Jumbulance with two drivers is costly. Some patients can afford to pay for themselves, others need to be funded. The helpers also have to pay about £400 each for the privilege of being a helper. Again, they might be paying for themselves or be sponsored. The UK tends to send most groups, each of which tends to be known by the name of the town it starts from. L'Astazou also receives groups from countries all over the continent. Jumbulance trips normally start on a Friday and cross the Channel via Dover, aiming to reach L'Astazou by noon on Saturday. The vehicle is then turned around and makes a return trip with a new crew to reach the town in England from which it started on Sunday afternoon. Normally every Jumbulance has a doctor and two nurses on board and patients have to produce a medical certificate to say they are fit to make the journey.

The leader of the first trip Ann Knox made on a Jumbulance was Kevin Dring, who later became a priest and was until recently secretary to Bishop Cormac. Ann then made several trips to L'Astazou as a nurse attached to the Brighton Jumbulance group. In subsequent years, after an operation for cancer, she decided to go as concierge in charge of one of the houses. When there are staff problems, or simply as holiday relief, Ann will fly out at her own expense and stay at L'Astazou for three weeks or three months. A concierge is responsible for the smooth running of the house, dealing with laundry, food, packed lunches, booking trips and transport, making sure medicines are stored properly and ready when needed, and the general care and comfort of residents.

The ACROSS season starts around Easter and ends in late October. November is usually the month for maintenance, re-decoration and repairs at L'Astazou before it closes down for the winter.

The Arundel and Brighton pilgrimage to Lourdes, which is an annual diocesan event lasting just one week, is not connected with ACROSS.

## A pilgrimage to Sutton Park . . .

In May 1984 thirty parishioners made a Holy Year pilgrimage to St Edward's Church, Sutton Park, near Guildford. This was one of four sites in the diocese selected as suitable for pilgrimage sites, the other three being the Church of Our Lady and St Francis, West Grinstead, the Church of Our Lady of Ransom, Eastbourne and Our Lady of England Priory, Storrington.

St Edward's Church stands on the site of the ancient manor of Sutton used by Edward the Confessor as a hunting lodge. Henry VIII granted it in 1521 to his favourite, Sir Richard Weston, who built a new mansion, Sutton Place, half a mile to the south. Mass was celebrated there during penal times and down the centuries. In the early 1800s a chapel was established in the mansion and the chaplain was put in charge of a 'mission' to serve Catholics scattered over a wide area.

In 1920 the Westons sold Sutton Place to the Duke of Sutherland who forty years later sold it to John Paul Getty, the oil billionaire. Getty spent the latter part of his life, and indeed died, there. After being owned by another American, Stanley Seeger, Sutton Place was until 1999 in the hands of Frederick Koch, whose art collection it housed. It was then placed on the market for £25 million but failed to attract a buyer. The property is now managed by the Sutton Place Foundation and open to visitors at certain times of the year. The parish church replaced the chapel on the site in 1876, hence the dedication to St Edward.

## . . . and to the Holy Land

A pilgrimage was made to the Holy Land at the end of September 1985 It is an area on which Father McSheehy was quite expert. An account of the ten-day tour, kept by the late Bernard Hurst, who came with his wife from Marlow to travel with their friends, Margaret and Pat Fallon, makes it possible to follow in the footsteps of the travellers, see what they saw – and wonder with them:

**DAY 2**

Drove round to the north and east of the Old City along the ridge of Mount Scopus, and then on to the Mount of Olives. We called into the Church of

Dominus Flevit, literally the 'crying of the Lord', on Maundy Thursday. Then up into the Old City through St Stephen's, or the Land, gate. Mass was celebrated at the Church of St Anne, manned by the French white fathers of Africa. This is substantially still a Crusader church with some nineteenth century additions by a French architect. It immediately adjoins the Pool of Bethesda, which is of ancient origin with a pagan temple at its southern end; water systems dating from the time of King Herod; and, at a higher level, the remains of another Crusader church.

Further into the City, the Via Dolorosa started, the first three stations being in the remains of the Fortress of Antonia. This included the Church of the Flagellation, and close by is the Ecce Homo Arch, reputedly the place where Pilate said 'Behold the man'. Several other stations were then passed in the very narrow streets of the Muslim quarter, the final four being in the Church of the Holy Sepulchre. This is a series of separate buildings of different ages and their use is shared by the various historic Christian faiths – Roman Catholic, Greek Orthodox, Coptic, Armenian and Egyptian. Incorporated within it is the reputed site of Calvary and the tomb in which Christ's body was laid afterwards. There was rather an unusual interlude at one o'clock when Greek, Armenian and Egyptian priests in succession went round incensing various altars and shrines within the church.

From Ein Karem, where we stopped at the birthplace of St John the Baptist, we went to Qubeiba, a village which is now entirely Muslim, but which is the Emmaus of the Gospel story. This area, among others, is under the control of the Franciscans, who several hundred years ago were given the responsibility of looking after most of the holy places.

**DAY 3**

To Bethlehem, ahead of the rush. Our first call was to the Church of the Nativity, a Greek Orthodox church of ancient origin and with a chequered history. There is an impressive approach to it through Manger Square, but an insignificant entrance which is barely wide enough for one person and involves almost bending double. As is often the case the existing building is well above the original site – here again in the crypt one finds the remains of the reputed original stable. Alongside is a much more modern and simpler church – again under the control of Franciscans – and it is from this that the traditional Christmas Eve/Christmas Day services are televised.

By coach to the Shepherds' Fields, where the angels reputedly appeared to shepherds at the first Christmas. A shrine has been made in of one of the caves in which shepherds would shelter, and Mass was celebrated there.

The Rottingdean pilgrims in Jerusalem.

Back to Jerusalem to Mount Zion, entering the Old City through the Dung Gate which gets its name from the fact that rubbish was brought in through this gate and dumped near the Western Wall. Being the eve of Yom Kippur hundreds of Jews, mostly Orthodox, were making their final visit for prayers and it was a hive of activity. We had to pass through a strict security check, and then a further check when we entered the Temple area which occupies the site of the original Temple and of the subsequent second Temple. It is now in Muslim hands and is their third holiest centre. We could not enter any of the buildings but they were most impressive, in particular the El Aksa Mosque, to the south of which had originally stood the money changers' hall, and the Dome of the Rock from where Muhammed is said to have ascended into Heaven.

The room of The Last Supper is a relatively modern, sixth or seventh century, building on what is said to be the original site. The Abbey of the Dormition, reputedly on the site of the place where Our Lady lived after the resurrection, is again a modern structure and in the care of German Benedictines.

Our last visit was to the Church of St Peter in Galicantu. This was within the City wall at the time of Christ, but is now outside, down a steep hill, and is on the site of one of the High Priest's houses. Alongside it there is an extensive stretch of a steep pathway, connecting Gethsemane with the room of The Last Supper. Yet again the church is relatively modern, but at its lowest levels one can see cells in which Our Lord might well have been kept, and scourged. This is where St Peter denied Our Lord three times before the cock crowed thrice, hence the name.

**DAY 4**

Today is the feast of Yom Kippur and there is little in the way of organised activities, as the Jewish law not only requires that no one should work, but also that one should not be using the products of other people's work, such as electricity. In the Old City, mainly in the Christian, but partly in the Muslim quarter, things were almost as normal and we were able to do some shopping, meeting again at the Jaffa Gate. Then we walked outside the City walls, the lower parts of which dated back to the time of Herod, and unintentionally re-entered through the Zion Gate when heading for the Western Wall. We were pleasantly surprised by how close we were able to get to the Wall, in front of which there were many thousands of people.

**DAY 5**

Got caught up in the Jerusalem rush hour traffic and arrived a little late at the Church of the Agony in Gethsemane for Mass. Then off eastwards and joined the Dead Sea almost at its northernmost point, just north of Qumran. We arrived at Massada, the site of Herod's fortress, where one Jewish sect, the Zealots, held out for some years after the Roman Conquest. Ultimately the survivors, rather than become slaves of the Romans, all committed suicide. Massada now forms almost as important a part of Jewish history as does the Holocaust.

**DAY 6**

To the Church of the Holy Sepulchre where Mass was said. Then another short journey to Ein Karem, and a stiff uphill climb on foot to the Church of the Visitation. Here one of the outside walls was covered with mural panels with the words of the Magnificat in almost every known language. Then back into the Old City for Stations of the Cross. We were off again in the evening to Bethlehem for an Arab meal, some shopping, and then a film on the life of Christ.

**DAY 7**

Went to Bethany, which is quite close to the Old City, being separated from it by the Mount of Olives. Mass was said in the church on the site of the house of Martha and Mary. We visited the tomb in which their brother Lazarus had lain dead for four days, before being brought back to life. Once again this is a relatively modern church on the site of an earlier Byzantine, and later Crusader, church.

We went almost to the Dead Sea and stopped briefly at a derelict desert inn, reputedly the one involved in the parable of the Good Samaritan, before turning north towards Jericho, the oldest city in the world, with a present population of some 12,000. After the barrenness of the wilderness, the lushness around Jericho was very striking.

Along the Israeli/Jordan frontier the land reclamation plans were much in evidence. Most of this area is what is now termed the West Bank which Israel has taken from Jordan. After a brief stop at the Kismeret kibbutz on the banks of the Jordan where it leaves the Sea of Galilee – there we saw some members of an obscure American sect from St Louis being baptized by total immersion – we returned to our hotel in Tiberius.

**DAY 8**

Boarded a boat to cross the Sea of Galilee to Capernaum, the home of St Peter and a place which was regularly visited by Christ. We went to the Church of the Primacy of St Peter for Mass. This is a relatively modern building, the sanctuary of which incorporates a rock, representing that to which Christ referred when saying: 'Thou art Peter and upon this rock. . .' Close by there was a natural amphitheatre, possibly similar to the place where, when preaching to a multitude, Christ got into a boat and pulled off-shore, and could still be heard. A short distance away was the Church of the Loaves and Fishes at Tabgha. Again this is a modern church, built in the 1950s by German Benedictines, but it is at least on the proven site of two earlier churches, one very early, and the other from about the fifth century. Numerous mosaics from the second church were discovered and have been incorporated into the structure. There was a fairly steep winding climb to the top of the Mount of the Beatitudes, the reputed site of the Sermon on the Mount.

The need for the Israelis to expel the Syrians from the Golan Heights became obvious today – the whole of Israel draws its fresh water from the Sea of Galilee, and the hidden pumping station is at its northern end, but was well within the range of shell fire from the Heights. On two occasions we thought that hostilities had broken out again, but it turned out that these were jet aircraft of one side or the other breaking the sound barrier.

**DAY 9**

We drove northwards, and then inland from the Sea of Galilee, climbing up to sea level, our first stop being in Cana. In the course of a brief visit to the church on the site of Christ's first miracle, those of us who were married renewed our marriage vows. Mass was said in the Basilica of the Annunciation, a 1958 church but again on the site of earlier buildings. In the crypt is the reputed site of the Annunciation. While Mass was still in progress there was some opposition from the amplified voices of the Muezzim from a nearby mosque.

We spent a few quiet minutes in the Chapel of the Little Sisters of Jesus of Nazareth, and subsequently visited the synagogue, now a Greek Catholic Church, in which Our Lord preached, and from which he was expelled by the mob. After a lunch stop at a kibbutz restaurant, we went to Mount Tabor, the site of the Transfiguration.

**DAY 10**

From Tiberius we drove through the valley of Israel, passing by Mount Tabor, to Haifa. This was virtually the first occasion on which we saw lush and fertile countryside. Haifa is the principal industrial centre of Israel. We skirted round the port and town, climbing to the lighthouse headland in the west, and then visited the Carmelite church, and the principal house of the Carmelites, on Mount Carmel, where Mass was said in the church that marks the traditional site of the cave of Elijah.

There is no central barrier or reservation on the first few miles of the coastal motorway through the Plain of Sharon so it can, in an emergency, be used as a temporary air strip. At Caesarea, built by Herod to rival Alexandria, excavations in recent years have revealed extensive works, but these apparently only comprise about one-tenth of the original city, which housed 120,000 people. In Roman times the port was taken over and extended, and it was here that Paul was held prisoner for two years.

At Tel Aviv we were allowed twenty minutes shopping and then taken to the airport where security was very strict. Our plane was delayed by about half an hour, but we returned safely to Gatwick and then by coach to Brighton.

It was a sad postscript to the pilgrimage that a number of the party had to be stretchered off the plane. Mercifully it was only at the end of the tour that anyone suffered from 'gippy timmy' in this way and the victims quickly recovered.

Another pilgrimage to the Holy Land, this time led by Father McSheehy's successor, Father Charles Jeffries, is scheduled for 2001.

## Church care and repair

Father Cyril Butler was a keen DIY man and in 1974 he enlisted a band of volunteers to redecorate the church. Syd Ward was one of them and during the day he painted the whole of the nave ceiling down to the

*Photo: Arthur Waine*

**When the interior of the church needed redecorating, willing volunteers undertook the work.**

top of the arches. In the evening another group of volunteers took over. Once there was a near-disaster. A borrowed gantry collapsed into the aisle as it was being erected to enable the volunteer painters to reach the canopy over the altar and give it a fresh coat of liquid gold. Fortunately no one was hurt and no lasting damage done.

The need for structural repairs to the church became apparent in 1980. Bunty Phillips organised a mini-market and coffeee morning which raised £288 towards the £2,500 needed to repair the roof inside and outside and replace the flashings. The organ was renewed for the jubilee at a cost of £1,500. A replacement would have cost about £25,000. The presbytery was renovated in 1984 and the following year Father McSheehy used his DIY skills and £20 worth of materials on the sun lounge outside the dining room at Eastfield, saving the parish the £400 that a professional had quoted for doing the work.

Extensive work was done on the church's heating system in 1985. It had never worked very satisfactorily and a new gas fired system which kept the building warm in winter and cool in summer was installed at a total cost of around £8,000. At the same time the windows were reglazed and re-sealed. There were problems with three large windows in a side aisle and some smaller ones needed replacing. This work, which involved re-setting and re-leading the windows on the south side, cost around £5,000.

When it was found that water was seeping in from the flat roof of the Lady Chapel, volunteers remedied the fault by applying a protective coating of silicone to the affected part of the exterior. In the October 1987 hurricane some of the roof tiles were lifted and some further remedial work was undertaken.

As with any building, maintenance work has to go on and on. Some minor repairs were needed in 1998 and in 1999 the north side of the nave roof needed attention to prevent rainwater building up and seeping into the church.

☆ ☆ ☆

# 12

# The end of a century

THE Parish Pastoral Council received a letter from parishioner Miss Gladys Gilles in November 1985 suggesting that a small hall, complete with toilet facilities, should be built in the presbytery grounds. The matter was fully discussed but at the time no action was taken. John Remers, then president of the local St Vincent de Paul Conference and secretary of the PPC, put the idea unofficially to Father McSheehy and found him initially opposed to the project. Later, however, his attitude would change to one of enthusiasm.

It was at a Renew meeting at Pax that the scheme was put to the parish priest outright. Mrs Ann Turner, whose telephone call to Canon José had rescued Rottingdean's RC primary school project, said simply 'What we need is a hall' and those at the meeting agreed with her. Faced with this strength of opinion, Father McSheehy deputed selected council members to investigate the matter more fully. John Derrington, a structural engineer and member of the Ideas Sub-Committee, took a keen interest in the project and helped to drive it forward. He approached Paris and Company, a firm with a virtual monopoly on diocesan building work, to obtain preliminary information from them and by mid-June 1990 he had the outline of a scheme to put to fellow members of the council.

There was to be a new entrance to the church from The Twitten, a new parish room, lavatories and a room for children. The latter was not in fact built.

Another member of the sub-committee, Malcolm Alcock, approached Clive Müdd, a professional architect, to enlist his services. By

**Artist's impression of the church and the new parish room viewed from The Twitten.**

December 1990 draft drawings, which provided also for a kitchen, were ready. The proposed premises would be able to accommodate up to fifty people and the estimated cost was £120, 000.

The following February it was agreed at the annual meeting that the cost needed to be reduced. A week later, the Ideas Sub-Committee, having done its work, was disbanded and a Working Group composed of John Derrington, John Remers, Neil Wallace and Clive Müdd was set up to consider how to put the proposals into effect if sufficient financial support was forthcoming.

Leaflets appealing for funds were distributed and when parishioners had promised finance approaching one-third, £19,000, of the revised anticipated cost of around £57,000, a Building Fund was set up. Once two-thirds of the total cost had been raised, building work could start. The balance would be met out of other parish funds. Paris Construction Ltd had prepared the building plan free of charge and offered to take care of seeking detailed planning permission for £2 500.

Towards the end of 1991, the plans had to be re-drawn to bring the proposed extension even nearer to the church, in line with the planning authorities' recommendations. When it was learned that Paris's revised

**Work on the parish room gets under way.**

estimate was £112,000, plus professional fees of £5,000, a question mark hung over the whole project. Substituting brick for flintwork on the exterior facing would save £7,000 and this economy was accepted, although Rottingdean Preservation Society was opposed to the change of materials.

The benefits of the new building were obvious. It would provide much improved access to the church, fire exit facilities, immediately available conveniences and catering facilities, a sheltered area for parishioners to mingle and talk, a venue for Traidcraft and for the sale or display of other goods as well as for children's liturgy and organisational/social activities at times when the school was in use. In general, it offered convenient alternative premises to the school for parish meetings and other gatherings.

In August 1991, an amended planning application was approved and the quotation from Paris was for £114 000, not including fitting out. This was still too high and, following a tender, a rival estimate was received from Taylor/Standing Associates of Peacehaven for £83,000 including furnishings.

Developments were now rapid. An appeal was launched for £60 000, of which £4,000 was already in the building fund and £16,000 had been promised. On the 16 March 1993, as a result of the generous response of the parish to this project, it was possible to sign an agreement with Taylor/Standing Associates for the contractual sum of £81,500 which included a £3,500 contingency. Clive Müdd, in the capacity of architect/contract administrator, signed below Father John McSheehy.

The building was formally opened in December 1993 by Bishop Cormac. Two years after construction, the short gap between the parish room and the church was closed, making it an integral part of the overall structure. A new entrance hallway and porch was created, offering easier access to the church, especially for the disabled. The final cost of the extension was around £100, 000 and was met through contributions from the parish and the diocese. Internal fittings were obtained at favourable prices from different sources and some were donated.

## The end of a ministry

In 1996, on the forty ninth anniversary of his ordination, Father John McSheehy attended an annual reunion of his fellow seminarians. By then, four of the original sixteen had already passed on. Talk was of retirement, although he himself was not keen. He would have been quite glad to retire from Renews and Visions, but he did not want to leave Rottingdean. His wish was to be granted.

His death on 11 August was completely unexpected. He was simply found dead in his chair, with a blanket over his legs and his two beloved cats on his knees. That day, a Sunday, he had celebrated the Masses as usual and his last pastoral duty had been a baptism in the afternoon.

In a moving homily, Canon John Stapleton, a friend and fellow-teacher, described him as 'one of those special people who are precious to the Church today, in the closing years of the twentieth century. . . who actively encouraged everyone to make their contribution. Partners in Service indeed'. Father Martin Morgan, the vicar of St Margaret's, Rottingdean, was on holiday in Brittany when he learned of the passing of Father McSheehy. Of his neighbour and friend he wrote:

'It was fitting that almost the last thing he did in this life was to officiate at that sacrament of new life – baptism. To hear him celebrate Mass was to witness someone who knew its reality. So much more evangelistic and authentic than a million or more of the gimmicks so besetting the church. He was a man of prayer and as someone in the village said 'he was a real gentleman'.

'He was a man who enjoyed a good table, as I witnessed at the convent, at Sister Maire's and I hope in this vicarage. We met together with the other clergy of the area and as guests of the sisters and on those occasions laughter came readily to his lips.

'While he was in no way to compromise his beliefs he was prepared to work together in ways to bring together the various Christians in the village. He and I were beginning to talk seriously about ways in which we could do more things together and certainly to examine ways in which we could celebrate the millennium as a Christian celebration which is not to be lost entirely to the secular. We especially wanted to look at Holy Week to see how liturgically we could do more joint things.

'Father John would have celebrated the Jubilee of his priesthood at the end of May next year. Fifty years of faithfulness to his calling. Sad for us that we shall not have that planned party but a joy for him that he is now with God, seated enjoying his place at the banquet which God promises. A humble parish priest and yet now a prince of the kingdom.'

Father McSheehy's Requiem Mass was concelebrated by many clergy from the diocese in Our Lady of Lourdes church. His simple headstone in the churchyard of St Margaret's records his age, seventy four, and bears the inscription 'Parish Priest of Our Lady of Lourdes, 1979-1996.'

## Parish organisations and causes

CAFOD, the Catholic Fund for Overseas Development, is the official overseas aid agency of the Catholic Church in England and Wales. It is one of the major relief and development agencies in the UK, helping people throughout the Third World to help themselves with the fullest local involvement regardless of race, religious beliefs or politics.

It was set up by the Bishop's Conference in 1962, and by 1972, it was helping to fund 245 self-help projects in forty countries. In that year the first journal was produced to introduce parishes in England and Wales to the organisation's work. From the outset, lay organisations such as the Union of Catholic Mothers and the Catholic Women's League had been helping with distributing literature and collecting money, especially for the Family Fast Day.

In 1981, new guidelines for the running of CAFOD were drawn up by the Bishops' Conference of England and Wales. In this parish, a project to help Brazilian farmers was started. In 1983 a joint service of dedication for the new directors of CAFOD and Christian Aid was conducted by Cardinal Basil Hume and Archbishop Robert Runcie. The next year saw the launch of Working in Partnership, linking groups in schools and parishes here with countries abroad where CAFOD supported development programmes, and of the Crisis in Africa appeal in response to the drought and famine situation on that continent. In November the Parish Pastoral Council sent £1,020 to the Ethiopian Famine Fund.

In September 1984, in response to Bishop Cormac's moving pastoral letter on conditions in Peru and especially the diocese of Chulucanas where three priests from Arundel and Brighton diocese were working, £300 was collected by Our Lady of Lourdes parishioners. The following year the Catholic community nationally raised nearly £5 million for the relief of famine in Africa. In Rottingdean the ongoing projects were raising funds for a jeep for Honduras and slum clearance in Kenya.

On 1 March 1995, Landmines Action was launched as part of the Refugee Campaign. In Rottingdean parish, a project in Mozambique was started in January and finished a year later. Another was then undertaken in Cambodia, where landmines had caused much disability and limb loss. CAFOD was training people who had been fitted with artificial limbs by other organisations. By mid-1996, £469 was raised in Rottingdean for the project, of which £273 came from the church collection and the balance from the monthly CAFOD coffee mornings, which each raised on average £24-30.

At the beginning of 1997, CAFOD's five-year plan was launched and more than 1,300 supporters helped to initiate its millennium campaign, *A Fair Deal for the Poor*. This deals with the unpayable debt owed by the poorest countries and the slave-like working conditions that are endured by many workers in the Third World.

## Traidcraft

Traidcraft is the largest independent fair trade organisation in the UK, and has been represented in the parish by Fair Traders, Brian and Ann Turner, since 1992.

It was set up to challenge the unfair way international trading systems are usually structured. Small businesses in Third World countries are disadvantaged commercially through, among other things, a lack of knowledge and resources. As a result, it is difficult for them to compete on world markets and to earn enough money to pay for adequate food, shelter, health care and education.

Traidcraft operates on the principle that by establishing long-term relationships of partnerships and cooperation and paying a fair price for the products we buy, we can help poor communities to work their way out of poverty and create a more equitable world. Most of the trading partners are community-based enterprises and associations of smallholder farmers organised for the benefit of their producers and growers. They are given access to credit to enable them to buy the raw materials they need. Training programmes which develop the skills and knowledge of the producers are also supported.

Traidcraft sells a range of fair trade products, including crafts, fashions, foods, beverages, paper and cards through an extensive network of Fair Traders, or representatives, as well as by mail order catalogue and a number of independent retail outlets. As an organisation, Traidcraft consists of Tradecraft plc, a trading company, and Traidcraft Exchange, its linked charity. The company provides a working model of fair trade within the commercial sector, while the Exchange works to promote fairer trading systems as a solution to Third Word poverty. It includes CAFOD among its supporters.

In November 1992, there was a phenomenal response to the Traidcraft Stall in the parish run by Ann and Brian. They began with £250 and planned that their sales should be a continuing feature of parish life. By March of the following year turnover had already exceeded £1,000. There was sustained support by parishioners for the initiative. In 1995/1996 they purchased some £1,900 worth of goods from Traidcraft, virtually all of which were sold, representing an average monthly sale of £160. The cumulative sales since the venture was started totalled nearly £7,000, mostly through the monthly sales. At Easter 2001 the Turners are taking a well-earned retirement from Traidcraft after nearly a decade of sustained service.

There has also been support from the village church, St Margaret's. In October 1995 it displayed and sold Traidcraft goods at a United Service, and also purchased a consignment of Café Direct to the value of £199 for use at coffee mornings. A talk on Traidcraft to St Margaret's Women's Group yielded sales of £80.84.

## The Guild of St Martha

When Father McSheehy came to the parish in 1979, he was surprised there was no women's group here. He therefore asked the late Mrs Marjorie Furner to look into the possibility of forming such a group with the twofold aim of creating a nucleus of women on whom he could call at any time for support and help and as a social circle for regular gatherings and activities. As a result the Guild of St Martha was founded with Mrs Marjorie Furner as its first chairman, Mrs Colette Wholey as secretary and Mrs Phyllis Chinn as treasurer.

The group had a membership of twenty to thirty and met monthly in a room at the convent, and occasionally in the presbytery. Benediction followed in the convent chapel. In later years it met at the Whiteway Centre. There were no subscriptions, membership being free to all.

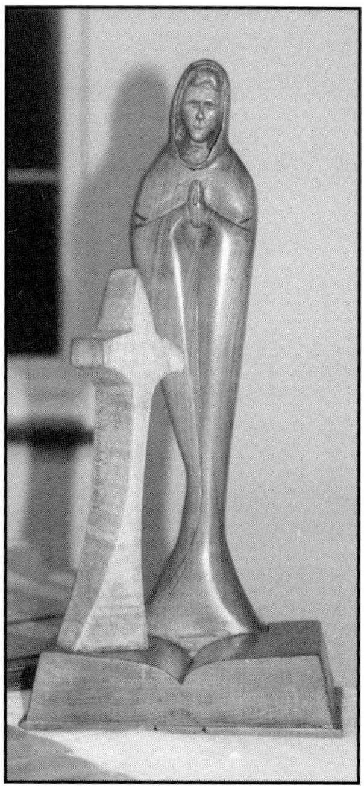

**The guild gave this wooden carving by Brian Turner of the Madonna to the parish room**

At its first Christmas the guild organised a coffee morning bring and buy at the convent for its adopted local charity, the St Thomas

Fund for the Homeless. The fund, operating from Cromwell Road, Hove, had been founded in the same year as the guild as a result of an initiative from the local Catholic community. It still provides accommodation and care for those made homeless as a result of alcohol or drug dependency and who have nowhere else to go. At that time it ran three, now reduced to two, short-stay centres in Hove and one in Portslade. In 1985 the guild sent it £200 and four years later the Sisters of St Martha's and the guild held a joint Ploughman's Lunch at the convent in aid of the St Thomas Fund and raised £190.

Marjorie Furner, who was also secretary of the Parish Pastoral Council, stayed at the helm until 1986, when she was replaced by Margaret Fallon. Although it had been well supported for many years attendances began to decline. Most of the members were now mainly of middle age and above. Younger women were occupied with jobs and families and were not free to attend guild meetings, which were held in the afternoon.

Gradually, because of the lack of support, the guild faded away. However, it has left behind a spiritual legacy in the form of the short meditation sessions, with readings and silent prayer, that are held under Margaret Fallon's leadership during Lent and Advent

## The 100+ Club

This steadily successful means of raising parish funds, suggested by parishioner John Knox, was started in 1980. It was an adaptation of a scheme operated locally by the Boy Scouts. This is how it works: Each annual 'share' costs £12 and parishioners can buy as many as they like. Each and every one is entered in a monthly draw for one of three prizes of £25, £15 and £10. Thus with a scheme operating with 100 shares, the annual income is £1,200 and the prize money is a constant of £600. The more shares sold in the year, the higher the profit ratio. In the club's history, this profit has ranged from just over £500 to £700. The scheme starts in July and the monthly prize draw takes place at the Sunday coffee morning after the 10.15am service.

When the club began in the parish, the number of shares sold was 150. Since then the number has ranged from ninety to 140. It should be noted that the number of shares does not equate to the number of supporting parishioners, since some purchase multiple shares.

In 1990, it continued to yield some £900 a year towards parish finances, while on 20 May 1991 it was stated to be 'continuing profitably despite predictions to the contrary.' In August that year it was 'launched again for the forthcoming year with fewer members but at an estimated annual profit of £600.'

In its fourteenth year the club's membership dropped from an average of 120 to 100 – thus lowering the profit margin – but the proceeds have remained an important source of parish funds. Since 1996, the scheme has been operated by Mrs Mary Brightwell. In 1999/2000 a total of 110 shares were sold, this being a fairly average figure.

## Co-Workers of Mother Teresa

In 1954, an Englishwoman named Ann Blaikie met Mother Teresa. She had heard of her rescuing a baby left in a dustbin and wanted to help her. She started finding people in Europe interested in the work of Mother Teresa and her young congregation of the Missionaries of Charity. Mrs Blaikie helped her with her first campaign in Calcutta to 'Touch a leper with your compassion'.

The Blaikie family returned to England in 1960. Nine years later, in Rome, Mrs Blaikie worked together with Mother Teresa on the constitution of what was to become the International Association of the Co-Workers of Mother Teresa. From 1974, the year her husband died, she started to travel all over to help the sisters and assist in organising the Co-Workers. In 1988 she retired in Surrey, still helping the young people who came to her for assistance. She died on 14 January 1996.

Mrs Pat Turner attended the first meeting to organise Co-Workers in Sussex which was held in Brighton.

The cause was taken up with enthusiasm in this parish, and a band of helpers led by Julia Getgood of Saltdean – it included the late Mrs Beryl Workman, also of Saltdean – gave many hours of their time to collecting materials and gifts to be dispatched to India's neediest.

Although Rottingdean parish's membership of the organisation ended in 1993, many Catholic and Anglican parishes throughout Sussex and nationally continue this important work of helping, housing, feeding, clothing and caring for the poor, thereby honouring Mother Teresa's memory.

## Ecumenical activities

A milestone in local ecumenism was represented by Contact 81, which brought local churches together in a way that no such initiative had ever done previously.

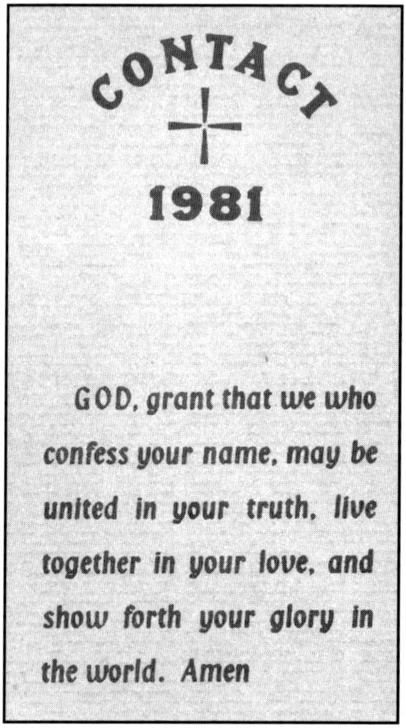


In October of 1981 a mission had been given by Father Vincent Lucas in Our Lady of Lourdes church and in the same period there were ecumenical services in the Anglican churches of Rottingdean and Ovingdean. Three successful ecumenical meetings were organised, with a final service at Longhill School, where Bishop Cormac's words greatly impressed all his listeners.

A joint tea party was held in the gardens of Rottingdean rectory and there were meetings of the clergy in Saltdean and Ovingdean.

The October 1986 issue of *LINK* reported on an open-air ecumenical event which had taken place a few weeks earlier:

'Bright sunshine preceded the Bank Holiday storms enabling the hundred or so members and friends of the three Saltdean churches to enjoy their 'out of doors' witness at the Saltdean Bowl.

Backed by an admirable band from the Salvation Army, there was some enthusiastic singing of favourite hymns led by Captain John Smith, with prayers by Father John McSheehy, and an excellent address from the Reverend David Clark . . . Unfortunately, despite the posters advertising the event, it was mainly a case of preaching to the faithful. People passed by and cast glances at the group of Christians gathered, but none showed enough interest to join in.

The snub of a youth carrying a blaring transistor radio seemed to personify the intolerance and disdain of public worship. Perhaps, to them, the gathering looked and sounded somewhat dull, and a more Bank Holiday type of meeting would have attracted more visitors?'

## The arrival of Father Charles Jeffries

The history of the parish begins a new chapter with the present parish priest, Father Charles Jeffries, coming to Rottingdean. He was not entirely unknown in this area as, in his capacity as Director of Religious Education, he had made a number of visits to Our Lady of Lourdes School in the 1970s.

Charles Jeffries was born in London in 1934. His father was on colonial service in Nigeria, where no white children were allowed, and rarely saw his son in his early years. Wilfred Jeffries ultimately became Superintendent of Adult Education for Northern Nigeria until his retirement at the age of fifty five.

Father Charles Jeffries

The infant Charles was sent to a nursery school almost at once, then a 'horrible' preparatory school, now closed, in south-east London. He went from there to Merchant Taylors School, near Watford. At the age of eleven he moved with his mother and sister to Worthing and five years later, when the family's circumstances changed, he went to stay with an uncle, a Presbyterian and a history master at Merchant Taylors.

In company with his new 'very wonderful' family, he attended their church and even became a Sunday School teacher. Yet he had never been baptised as his parents thought he should be allowed to make his own choices.

Charles enlisted for National Service and won a commission in 1952 in the Royal Army Service Corps. He applied for a posting to the Far East – and was sent to Dorset. There he served in a training battalion. After leaving the Army, he became engaged but the relationship ended. He then worked as a clerk, and later an inspector, for the Phoenix Assurance Company in the West End.

While there, he was instructed in the Catholic faith by Father Michael

Hollings, who was then on the staff of Westminster Cathedral. On the last day of 1957, he was baptised at the cathedral by Father Michael, to the great chagrin of his parents.

For the next six months he worked for the Sue Ryder Foundation and the United Nations in Germany helping refugees build their own homes near Hanover. When these operations were transferred to Austria he continued the work in different locations. It was while he was in Austria that he decided to become a priest.

On his return to England, he would tell Father Hollings every month of his resolve to take holy orders and would be told in reply that he had not been a Catholic long enough and should get a job. This Charles did, working in Peek Frean's biscuit factory in Bermondsey for three months and after that as a supply teacher at a local school.

By this time, he resolved to make no further reference to his vocation when he saw Father Hollings. As he was leaving after his next visit, his mentor turned to him and said: 'Have you ever thought of becoming a priest?'

Pre-seminary training followed at Campion House, Osterley, a late vocations house run by the Jesuits. There Charles resumed his studies of Latin, English, French and Greek. From there he went to St John's Seminary, Wonersh. As part of his training, he was sent out to Englefeld Green, near Staines, as a deacon, an experience he greatly enjoyed. This was the first year this scheme had been introduced and the seminary staff often wondered whether their charges would come back. In 1967, when he was living in Faygate, he was ordained at St John the Evangelist Church. Horsham.

One of his apprehensions about his vocation was that he would have to give up his beloved birdwatching and travelling, yet he has been able to do more of both than he would probably otherwise have done. The ordination present from his family was a pair of binoculars, and almost as soon as he took his vows, he was asked to go as the Catholic chaplain on an educational cruise round the Mediterranean.

His first position was as curate at the church of the Sacred Heart in Cobham. At Easter following his ordination he was pressured into going to Lourdes. He reluctantly accepted yet established such a good rapport with the children on the trip that he went a further nineteen times. When he had been a priest for five years, Bishop Michael Bowen asked him to go and train to take charge of religious education in the diocese. He studied for a year at Corpus Christi College, Notting Hill. It was some compensation that in the Easter holidays he was able to persuade the bishop to pay for a trip to the Holy Land.

As Director of the Religious Education Service for the diocese of Arundel and Brighton, he lived for five years in Ashdown Forest, serving with two other priests and supplying with them for other priests in the area. For four years prior to coming to Rottingdean, he was at West Grinstead attending to the welfare and ongoing formation of the diocese's clergy and looking after the parish and the Church of Our Lady of Consolation and St Francis.

Here Hilaire Belloc, who lived in the parish for almost fifty years and worshipped regularly at the church, is buried. Here too pilgrims are attracted to the shrine of Our Lady. Hidden among the rafters of the timbered presbytery is a secret chapel built after the Gunpowder Plot. It contains the relics of the Venerable Francis Bell, who in 1643 was martyred at Tyburn after giving himself up to save three young priests.

The West Grinstead church and presbytery and, of course, the priest, were featured in a series of articles on churches in *The Times* in 1997. In her five-star guide Ruth Gledhill awarded four points each for the architecture, the music, the 'spiritual high' and after-service care – coffee, wine and the tour of the priest's house. For his sermon, described as 'gently humorous,' Father Charles was awarded the maximum five stars. At the same time as that feature appeared, official word of his appointment to Our Lady of Lourdes church reached Rottingdean. When he arrived, he was greeted by Ann and Brian Turner reminding him that five-star sermons were expected in future. It would be fair to say that that expectation has been fulfilled.

Father Charles, who is currently a member of the College of Consultors and on the Board of the Southwark Brethren Charity for the relief of priests in conditions of need or hardship, was formally welcomed to the parish at a meeting of the Parish Pastoral Council on 2 April 1997. The chairman, John Remers, reminded members that it had been seven long months before the appointment had been made and warmly thanked all the clergy and the Sisters of St Martha for their help in keeping the parish going during that time. One priest who helped was

Father Jack O'Shea, a familiar figure in the parish for years, who, despite 'retiring' more than once, has yet remained in our midst, celebrating several masses in any given week. The Mass for the Solemn Induction of Father Charles took place on Saturday, 3 May 1997, at which the Dean, Father Anthony Churchill, officiated.

One major administrative change he made during his first year was to disband the Parish Pastoral Council and replace it in January 1998 with a Parish Team representing such various functions as Social Concerns, Justice and Peace, Marriage and Family Life, Catechetics, Social Activities, Ecumenical Adult Education and Liturgy, Youth, Small Groups, Convent and School. There are now parish meetings twice a year at which anyone present can speak and vote.

## St Martha's Convent

Far from declining into inactivity after the closure of its school more

**The Sisters of St Martha enjoy refreshments with Father O'Shea at the Whiteway Centre. Seated: Sister Mary Patrice from St Martha's, Falkirk; Father O'Shea; Sister Margaret; Sister Philippe de Neri from France. Standing: Sister Bernadette, Falkirk; Sister Cécile, St Martha's, Hadley Bourne, and Sister Pauline.**

**Sister Pauline and Sister Margaret of St Martha's Convent, Rottingdean, pictured on the parish's pilgrimage to Canterbury Cathedral in preparation for the Millennium.**

than thirty years ago, St Martha's Convent continues to offer hospitality to the religious, the lay and also to those who wish to make a private retreat. It has quite a number of new guests each year as well as its faithful regulars who have been coming many years running. To the best of their ability Sister Pauline and Sister Margaret, the two nuns remaining at the convent, create for them comfortable conditions and a peaceful environment in the hope that their spiritual life and their physical needs will be catered for and renewed.

The convent offers a choice of accommodation in its 'holiday house for ladies'. There are comfortable single bedrooms with hot and cold water, two of which are on the ground floor, and there are two cottages in the convent grounds, one with three bedrooms, the other with two. These are available from Saturday to Saturday in the summer season and the illustrated brochure advises early application by guests 'who do not require nursing or medical attention or extra special diets'.

## Forty years on – a ruby anniversary

The fortieth anniversary of the consecration of the Church of Our Lady of Lourdes, Queen of Peace, was celebrated on 10 September 1998. Since

**Clergy and congregation process past the pond on their way to a service marking the fortieth anniversary of Our Lady of Lourdes, Queen of Peace.**
*Photo: John Knox.*

**The ruby anniversary display set up by the author in the parish room.**

a handful of exiled Sisters of St Martha brought the Catholic faith back to Rottingdean in 1903, the convent on The Green was an appropriate starting point for the long procession, which brought traffic to a halt as its wound past the pond to the church.

'There is some satisfaction in holding up the traffic for once to make way for reflection and praise', said Bishop Cormac in his homily.

During the service, four young parishioners offered up items symbolising the various stages in the construction of the church. From Siobhan O'Hara there was money, from Emma Griffiths a plan, from David McGovern a downland flint and from Martin Tyler a hammer.

Among the clergy at the service were Canon Seamus Hester, Dean of Brighton and Hove, Father Martin Morgan of St Margaret's, Rottingdean and Father Paul Turner. There were sisters from St Martha's Convents and one member of the Order who had made the journey from the Mother House in Périgueux.

There was a potted history of the parish in the service booklet and an exhibition in the parish room illustrated the highlights of the church's first forty years with photographs, drawings and text.

## A window for Our Lady

A strikingly beautiful stained-glass Millennium window was unveiled in the gallery of the church on the feast of Our Lady of Lourdes, 11 February 2000, by the Earl of Lytton. It was designed by Rosalind Sprey and constructed by Opus Stained Glass of Poynings. It was given to the church through the generosity of two anonymous donors.

Among the 150 or so at the unveiling ceremony were children from the church's primary school, six of whom processed from the altar after the reading, each carrying a multi-coloured heart-shaped banner with the words of Mary and Bernadette in equal number:

**'My soul glorifies the Lord',**
**'The Almighty works marvels for me. Holy is His Name',**
**'Behold, the handmaid of the Lord',**
**'I shall not live an instant without loving',**
**'The Cross is the tree of life – the mysterious ladder which links heaven to earth'**
**'I fear nothing because I have always told the truth.'**

The 5th Earl of Lytton, a chartered surveyor from Horsham and a

**The Millennium window, depicting Bernadette at the Grotto. The servers are Dominic Ryan and Harry Farmar.** *Photo: John Knox.*

Catholic born and bred, had known Father Charles Jeffries from his days as parish priest of the Church of Our Lady of Consolation and St Francis in West Grinstead. The dedication of the window was, he said, an act of great piety and a public testimony of faith by the community.

After the Lourdes hymn the parishioners, in small contingents, were able to go up to the gallery to view the window for themselves.

In the evening Bishop Cormac blessed the window and concelebrated the church's patronal feast with Father Kevin Dring, his secretary; Father Kevin Steen from Woodingdean; and Father Paul Turner from St Joseph's, Brighton.

Archbishop Cormac wrote the foreword to this parish history. It is fitting that he should have the last word too – and they are words of perceptive wisdom. In the course of an address on 'Church and Politics' given at Lewes in 1979 he identified the role of the parish and its community.

'I think there is a difference between the Church as it existed thirty years ago and the Church today,' he said. 'In past times, the Catholic Church of this country has been very much on the periphery of the social and political life, both locally and nationally. It is not so now and I think we should rejoice in it and realise that every Catholic has a part to play in local and national life'.

In Rottingdean village, this has been made possible by the Church of Our Lady of Lourdes. Let us thank God for this gift.

☆ ☆ ☆

# APPENDIX I

## CATHOLICS IN ROTTINGDEAN 1918-1925

A list of all the Catholics in Rottingdean in the years 1918 to 1925 was compiled by the ever-observant Marie-Thérèse Magee. She gives the briefest of details about the people concerned (shown in bold type) to which further information ascertained by the author has been added:

**AVERY, two sons, two daughters, Luly and Lucy, 1 son lost at sea, 1 came back. Father Dreves, Mme Achard and daughter stayed with them in Nevill Road, then at Holmbury, High St, then The Whim (St Ives), Steyning Road, till 1925**

'Luly' was Edith Avery who married local historian Henry T Smith. In fact the Averys had only one son, Bill, and he survived his Second World War naval service.

**BURROW, Mr and Mrs S, Shepherd, Nevill Road**

This is clearly a reference to Steve Barrow and his wife. He was one of the five shepherds employed by William Brown of Challenors towards the end of the nineteenth century. He was a great storyteller, and a great singer of local ballads as well. Given any encouragement at all at a village festivity, he would get up and sing verse after verse, while accompanying himself on a concertina.

He looked upon Rudyard Kipling as his rival. The fact that Kipling was then one of the greatest poets and storytellers in the world did not greatly impress him. His main worry was that Kipling, being in the same line of business, so to speak, might try and steal some of his material. For this reason he would never tell any of his famous stories in Kipling's hearing. 'That Rudyard Kipling', he would mutter darkly, 'would be sendin' em to Lunnon and makin' a mort of money out of 'em.'

His greatest anecdote, with which he used to chill the spines of all who heard it, was of how he had seen the last public hanging in England on a gibbet outside Lewes Gaol. He died in 1926 at the age of eighty one, having only a few months previously persuaded a pilot to take him up in an aeroplane and loop the loop with him.

Steve Barrow, as 'old Bramble', was the inspiration for the poem by

Alfred Noyes, entitled *The Silver Crook:*

> How should I paint Old Bramble – the shrewd face
> Brown as the wrinkled loam, the bright brown eyes,
> The patriarchal beard, the moleskin cap.

**COATES, Mrs, one daughter, became Matron of Guy's Hospital**
Mrs Frances Radcliffe Coates was a Sunday School teacher. She died in 1966 at the age of seventy nine. On her headstone in the churchyard there is a reference to a son who died two days later in an Air India disaster over Switzerland. Her husband was a master at St Aubyn's School and a great cricket fan.

**COURNIER, Mme, Chef, Steyning Road**

**CURTIS, Miss, companion**
According to Joyce Edwards, Bob Copper's sister, Miss Curtis, may have been the manageress of The Creamery.

**DONOGHUE, Steve, very successful jockey and family. Sweepstakes for all the big races. Many men were employed as grooms, etc. – racegoers overflowed into the village. Round the corner from the Doctor's house was a house with stables and fields where Steve Donoghue the Jockey trained Epsom winners. His was one of the R.C. families. He was very funny at Mass as he always knelt on his large silk hanky, which matched his tie, though the kneelers were very clean. In Steyning Road you could hear the strings of horses going up the road at back of the houses leading to the Downs and the Gallops – they were marked out with hurdles. Several large houses had stables and of course some of the villagers were stable lads, which meant they could always run a successful sweepstake in all the big races – the only time all had interests in common! We won several times!! Epinard, Cinderella, Sansovino. . .**

Stephen Donoghue was champion jockey each season from 1915 until 1923 and 'Come on, Steve' became a catchphrase of the age. He won his first Derby on Humorist in 1921, winning again the following year on Captain Cuttle and in 1923 on Papyrus. The squire of Telscombe village, Ambrose Gorham, used to keep his greyhounds and harriers at the The Paddock, Rottingdean, which still stands as No 46 in the aptly-named Gorham Avenue. During his tenancy of the premises, he was joined there for two years by Donoghue.

**Hairdresser and wife and one son, High St**
This was barber George Adkins, see page 22.

**HENNESSY, Mrs, widow, lived with two daughters, one son-in-law and two granddaughters (Mr and Mrs Sanders [Sandever], Noonie and Isobel)**
The family history of the Hennessys is fully detailed in Chapter 2 and there are frequent other references throughout the book to the Sandever sisters, Isabelle and Nonie.

**LEWES, Sir George Lewes and Lady Marie, one son and two daughters**
Sir George James Graham Lewis (1868-1927) was the son of the first baronet, Sir George Lewis, who had one of the most famous law practices in Victorian England. He and his family lived at The Grange, a large house facing the village pond, which they had purchased from the painter William Nicholson in 1914. George Lewis was in fact a Jew. His daughter Elizabeth became a Catholic. In her autobiography, Enid Bagnold wrote of her:

> 'She stood out from her family like a rock on a hillside. She had long been a Catholic – the loved convert of that group Belloc, Chesterton and Maurice Baring'.

Following the death of her husband, Lady Marie suffered bouts of insanity. She died in 1931. For the next five years The Grange was owned by her son, Sir George James Ernest Lewis. He sold it to Dorothy Neville, wife of Charles Neville, who founded Peacehaven and went on to develop Saltdean and parts of Rottingdean, including Dean Court Road and the former Tudor Close Hotel.

**MULLINS, Mr and Mrs, two sons, one daughter, Steyning Road**

**MURPHY, Mrs, widow, one daughter, one son-in-law, two grandsons.**
See Chapter 1 for details of the 'Murphy'/Furlong family. The son-in-law was Adkins the barber.

**NONSOTTI, Mr and Mrs, three girls**

**PENSOTTI, Mr and Mrs, one son and one daughter**
Mrs Magee noted elsewhere 'The Solicitors, the Pensottis, sold their large house to the Nuns to run as a Guest House 1931/32.' See page 49.

**ROTHERHAM, Lord and Lady**

Occupied a house named Lothersdale in Steyning Road. They had their own private chapel in the house, permission for which was granted to Lady Rotherham by Bishop Amigo in an Indult dated 11 February 1920. She was allowed to have one daily Mass celebrated in her presence, with no day in the year being excluded. It could be said by any properly approved secular priest or by any religious with the permission of his superior provided the parochial rights were safeguarded. Communion could be given to all 'relatives, guests and domestics, as well as the Mass-server.' Should a priest come to the house as a guest, a second Mass was allowed. Street directories indicate that Lothersdale became Half Way House and that therefore Maurice Baring took over the chapel.

**STACEY, Mr and Mrs, two sons, two daughters**

Mrs Stacey used to be a Sunday School teacher. She lost her husband during the First World War and one of her sons in the Second. The family lived in Dean Court Road.

**STEYNING, Mr and Mrs, two daughters**

Ernie Stenning was the last blacksmith in the village. John Leech remembers he 'swore like a trooper' while Wilf Jepson 'couldn't imagine him being a Catholic', nor was he. John lived next door to Ernie's assistant, Fred Hearn, in Park Crescent and then moved to the top of Nevill Road, where his next-door neighbour was Ernie himself. By contrast to Ernie, Mrs Stenning and her daughters, Margaret and Janet, were genteel. They were the Catholics in the family. The girls both went on to be Brighton councillors.

**THOMPSET, Mr and Mrs, and daughter**

**WEBSTER, Dr and Mrs, one son, three daughters**

Dr Webster lived in Court House. The road which slopes up north of The Green to the beginning of the Falmer Road is still known to some older locals as Doctor's Hill. On his re-marriage he lived in Steyning Road.

# APPENDIX II

## CHOIR REPERTOIRE 11.1.76–2.1.94

### Masses – Latin

*Our Lady of Buckfast.* D Godwin Forster
*St Cecilia.* Turner
*Venite Sanctus Spiritus.* Terry
*St Dominic.* Terry
*St Francis of Assisi.* Hilben
*St Gregory.* Griesbacher
*Short Mass.* Thomson
PLAINSONG MASSES
*Cum Jubilo*
*Mass XVII* (Lent and Advent)
*Missa de Angelis*
*Orbis Factor*
*Requiem*

### Masses – English

*Of Our Lady.* John Rush
*Of St David.* Alan Rees and Anthony Milner
*New People's Mass.* Dom Gregory Murray
*Of Blessed Sacrament.* Colin Mawby
*A People's Mass.* Wilfred Trotman
*For All Saints.* Joan McCrimmon
*Pope John.* Eric Welch
*Congress Mass.* Alan Rees
*Responsorial Mass.* Donald Whitehead and Derek Fry
*Of St Francis.* Philip Green
*Catholic Renewal Eucharist.* Leonard West
*The St Luke's Setting.* Victor Whitburn
*The Addington Service.* Richard Shephard

### Motets – Latin

*The Shrewsbury Mass.* Paul Inwood
*Ave Maria.* Flor Peters
*Ave Maria.* Franz Abt
*Ave Maria.* Arcadelt.
*Ave Maria.* Vittoria
*Ecce Sacerdos Magnus.* Stadler
*Jesu Rex Admirabilis.* Palestrina
*O Bone Jesu.* Palestrina
*Sacerdotes Domini.* Palestrina
*Panis Angelicus.* César Franck
*Cibarit Illos.* Christopher Tye
*O Sacrum Convivium.* Farrant
*Ave Verum.* Mozart
*Jubilate Deo.* Mozart
*Ecce Panis Angelorum.* Portuguese
*Ave Verum.* Elgar
*Ave Verum.* Byrd
*Ego sum pastor bonus.* Rombaut
*Haec Dies.* Rombaut
*Veni Sancte Spiritus.* MM 76

### Motets – English

*If I your Lord and Master.* (Maundy Thursday)
*Blessed City.* (Westminster Abbey)
*O Love that will not let me go.* A L Prach
*O Wondrous Love.* Bach
*Gracious Lord of all our being.* Bach
*Hail True Body.* J Dykes-Bower
*The Supreme Sacrifice*
*Can there be one.* Tchaikowsky
*Easter Carol*
*O taste and see.* R V Williams
Selected hymns from *Praise the Lord*
*Prayer of St Richard of Chichester.* L J White
*Teach us good Lord*
*I vow to thee my country*
*Come unto him.* Handel
*He shall feed his flock.* Handel
*On Eagle's Wings*
*Sing of the Lord's goodness.* MM 75
*Water of Life.* MM 64
*A Tryst of Love.* MM 111
*God be in my head.* John Rutter
*The Father's Love.* Simon Lole
*Hymn to the Holy Spirit.* Martin How
*Brother James' Air.* Marosa

# APPENDIX III

## Names on the memorial tablets in the church's Garden of Remembrance as at 5 January 2001

| NAME | DATE BORN | DATE DIED | DETAILS |
|---|---|---|---|
| Adams, Joyce F | Not shown | 5.5.99 | |
| Bridson, Eric | 30.4.1897 | 11.10.82 | |
| Bridson, Valerie | 20.4.1903 | 2.12.99 | |
| Bush, Ellen May | 2.7.1912 | 24.3.93 | |
| Callinan, Christina | Not shown | 14.3.1996 | |
| Carr, Mary M | 23.3.1917 | 15.2.1994 | formerly Wood |
| Carr, Patrick J | 27.4.20 | 1.4.90 | |
| Crow, Douglas | 1907 | 1990 | |
| Crow, Marguerite | 1905 | 1990 | |
| Day, Lilian | Not shown | 25.4.94 | |
| Finlan, Lilian | 22.8.06 | 2.9.97 | |
| Finlan, Martin | 22.7.06 | 13.10.87 | |
| Flanagan, Jack | Not shown | 25.3.95 | aged 74 |
| Gilles, Clementine | 23.7.1894 | 14.5.87 | |
| Gorman, Francesca | 1925 | 1990 | |
| Hardingham, Ken | 6.6.26 | 16.4.88 | |
| Hardingham, Mary | 6.1.26 | 16.4.88 | |
| Harris, Frederick | 1920 | 1997 | |
| Harris, Norah | 1917 | 1998 | |
| Hitchin, Albert | 1906 | 1990 | |
| Jalie, Mary Therese | 1909 | 1992 | |
| Lloyd, William | Not shown | 1996 | aged 79 |
| Morant, Selina Ann | Not shown | 7.12.95 | aged 87 |
| Muir, Phyllis | 1908 | 1998 | |
| Oldham, Edwin George | 1911 | 1990 | |
| Petty, Mary Jane | 1912 | 1998 | |
| Raffield, Bill | 1921 | 1999 | |
| Ruocco, Ben | 31.5.1925 | 2.3.90 | |
| Spalding, Kenneth Charles | 12.4.28 | 25.1.92 | |
| Stockton, Rose Pauline | 1898 | 1990 | |
| Turner, Garrett John | 18.11.1953 | 12.12.87 | |
| Wallace, Josephine | 1912 | 1997 | |
| Ward, Margarethe | 31.12.1899 | 18.7.87 | |
| Wells, Kathleen | Not shown | 1997 | aged 73 |

# BIBLIOGRAPHY


*A and B News*, November 1994.

*Arundel and Brighton Diocesan Directory*, 2001 and prior.

BAGNOLD, Enid, Enid Bagnold's Autobiography. William Heinemann, London, 1969.

BALLESTRERO, Anastasio, *Martha and Mary - Meeting Christ as Friend*, St Pauls, Slough, 1994.

BARING, Maurice, *The Puppet Show of Memory*, William Heinemann, London, 1922.

BERTRAM, Father Jerome, *History of Frimley Church.*

*Bible Alive*, Bible Alive Ltd, September 1997.

BIBLE. *The Jerusalem Bible*, Darton, Longman and Todd, London 1966

BLYTH, Henry, *Smugglers' Village – The Story of Rottingdean*, H E Blyth

BRIDSON, Michael, *The Building of All Saints Church, Oxted* in *The Oxted Review*, May 1998.

*Catholic Directory*, Gabriel Press, Manchester. Various years consulted.

CHESTERTON, G K, Autobiography, Hutchinson, London, 1937.

*Chesterton Review*, Maurice Baring special issue. Vol xix, No 1, February 1988.

*Chronicle of the 20th Century*, Longmans, London 1988.

*Church of Saint Thomas More, Seaford*. Parish Booklet. nd.

COPPER, Bob, *Early to Rise*, William Heinemann, London 1976 and *A Song for Every Season*, William Heinemann, London 1971.

CROSS, F L and LIVINGSTONE, E A (Eds.), *The Oxford Dictionary of the Christian Church*, Oxford University Press 1977.

CRYSTAL, David (Ed.), *Cambridge Biographical Encyclopaedia*, Cambridge University Press 1994.

d'ENNO, Douglas, *The Saltdean Story*, Phillimore, Chichester 1985.

d'HARCOURT, Anne-Pierre, *The Real Enemy*, Longmans, Green and Company, London 1967 and *Journal de Buchenwald* (November 1943-April 1945), compiled by Comtesse Laurian d'Harcourt. Privately printed, Buzançais, France 1988.

DREVES, Rev F-M, M.H.M., *With the Help of Our Lady*, Sands and Company, London and Glasgow 1965; *A Joyful Herald of the King of Kings and other Stories*, Sands and Company 1920;. *Remembered in Blessing (The Courtfield Story)*, Catholic Publishing Company 1955 for St Joseph's Missionary Centre, Courtfield, Ross-on-Wye; *Spreading the Faith*, St Joseph's Society for Foreign Missions, London *c*1923; and *Our Pilgrimage in France*, Sands and Company 1924.

*Encyclopaedia Britannica*, Britannica CD 2.0, 1995.

FARMER, David H (Ed.), *Oxford Dictionary of Saints*, Oxford University Press 1997.

FITZHUGH, Terrick V H (Revised Lumas, S), *The Dictionary of Genealogy*, 5th Edn, A and C Black, London 1998.

HARVEY, Andrew J, Rottingdean, *1841-1851 The Development of a Sussex Village*, dissertation, 1993.

HEATER, Derek, *The Remarkable History of Rottingdean,* Dyke Publications, Brighton 1993.
JULYAN, Herbert E, *Rottingdean asd the East Sussex Downs and Villages,* Lewes Press.
LETLEY, Emma, *Maurice Baring – A Citizen of Europe,* Constable,London 1991.
*LINK* magazine, various issues.
Logbook of Our Lady of Lourdes First School, 1969 to 1994.
MOENS, S M, *Rottingdean, The Story of a Village,* John Beal and Son, Brighton 1953.
MONTFORD, Selma, POLLARD, Jacqueline and SANDERSON, Robert, *The Vanishing Villas of Preston and Withdean,* Brighton Books (Publishing) 1996.
MORRIS, Betty, *The Story of a Parish – St Mary's, Preston Park, Brighton.* Booklet
MORTIMER, Roger, ONSLOW, Richard, WILLETT, Peter, *Biographical Encyclopedia of British Flat Racing,* McDonald and Jane's Publishers, London 1978.
MURPHY-O'CONNOR, Cormac, *The Family of the Church,* Darton, Longman and Todd, London 1984
MUSGRAVE, Clifford, *Life in Brighton,* New revised and enlarged edition, Rochester Press, Rochester 1981 (first published by Faber and Faber 1970).
*New Catholic Encyclopedia, Vol. XIV,* Catholic University of America, Washington, Dist. Columbia, McGraw-Hill Book Company, New York 1967
O'SHEA, Gerry, *History of the Church of the Immaculate Conception, Peacehaven, East Sussex* (unpublished draft, 1999).
Parish Pastoral Council Minutes, 1977-1997 (two volumes).
*The Parishioner,* Vol XIII, No 2, Brighton.
PARKER, Peter (Ed.), *The Reader's Companion to Twentieth Century Writers,* Fourth Estate Publishing, London and Helicon Publishing, Oxford 1995.
PUGH, Trevor, *The Church of St John the Baptist, Brighton, 1835-1985,* Brighton, published by St John the Baptist Church, Bristol Road, Brighton.
Rottingdean Preservation Society. Miscellaneous archives.
ROWLAND, David, *The Brighton Blitz,* S.B. Publications, Seaford 1997.
SEBBA, Anne, *Enid Bagnold,* Weidenfeld and Nicholson, London 1986.
SMITH, Michael, *The Grange – A Brief History of a House and its Residents,* Rottingdean Preservation Society 1994.
*Southwark Record* (official monthly organ of the Diocese of Southwark), Various issues from 1922.
THORNTON, Michael, *The New Roman Catholic Church at Rottingdean.* Article in *Downland Review* 1960.
THURSTON, Herbert, SJ, and ATTWATER, Donald (Eds.), *Butler's Lives of the Saints,* Vol. III, July, August, September, 1956 (first – this edition revised and supplemented), Burns and Oates.
TRIMINGHAM, Adam, *In Praise of Sussex Beauties,* a feature on Belloc in the *Weekend Argus,* July 2000.
WARD, Maisie, *Gilbert Keith Chesterton,* Penguin Books, 1958.
WARD, Margaret, *Memories of Rottingdean, 1920-1945,* QueensPark Market Books. 1993 and *One Camp Chair in the Living Room,* QueensPark Book No 19. 1988.

# ACKNOWLEDGMENTS

I am indebted firstly to Father Charles Jeffries, parish priest of the church, for consenting to the writing of this history and for making key records available, often at short notice. His interest and encouragement throughout the course of the project were a great support.

My warmest thanks go to Archbishop Cormac O'Connor, formerly Bishop of Arundel and Brighton, for readily agreeing, despite the tremendous pressures on his time, to write the Foreword.

I was greatly assisted in my early researches by the late Florence K Hulme of Rottingdean, who provided me with much material concerning Father O'Brien and the early plans to build the church.

I am grateful to Susan Rowland for two maps in this book and special thanks to my son, Neal, for the meticulously-drawn title page picture. Thanks also to James Gardner and Professor Hugh Drake, who read the manuscript and made helpful suggestions and comments.

When I returned to the project from late 1997 onwards, the following, listed alphabetically by surname where applicable, provided substantial help. Many of them granted me interviews, which I taped or otherwise recorded.

Malcolm Alcock; Miss Adèle Aldridge; Mrs Anne Allinson; Mrs Anne Austin; Peter Bailey (Curator, Newhaven Historical Museum); Mrs Peggy Bennets; Mrs Patty Bishop; Alan and Mrs Joan Bond (Catholic Central Library, London); John Boon; Fr Martin Breen, Frimley; Michael Bridson, Oxted; Anthony Brockhurst; Mrs Mary Browne; Joseph Bryce; Mrs Rosemary Buchan; Christopher Bussy; Peter Bussy; Roy and Mrs Pauline Butler; CAFOD, London; Mrs Honoria Campbell; Keith Campbell; Gillian Collings, former Acting Head, Our Lady of Lourdes School, Rottingdean; Mrs Barbara Cooper; Bob Copper; Howard and Mrs Marion Creighton; Mme la Comtesse Laurian d'Harcourt; Felice and Mrs Sheila De Rosa; Giulia De Rosa; Mrs Patricia 'Paddy' Dixon; Father Gerald Dunne of St Joseph's College, Mill Hill; Ken Eborn; Mrs Joyce Edwards; Mrs Margaret Fallon; Mrs Catherine Ferrers; Mrs Collette Flanagan; Father David Foley (St John the Baptist's, Kemp Town); Mrs Breda M Ford, general secretary of the Catholic Women's League; Mrs Sandra Funnell; Mrs Julia Getgood; Ms Brenda Gwyer. John Hale; Nick and Mrs Marion Hart; Andrew Harvey; John and Mrs M Jean Harvey; Mrs Patricia Hawkins; Father William O Heaney (St Mary's, Brighton); Edgar and Mrs Jean Hilder; Mrs Anne Holberton; Mrs Margaret Holt; Mrs Pamela Holt;

the late Miss Yvonne Hope; Mrs Elaine Haworth; Mrs Paddy Hughes; Monsignor Canon John Hull (Vicar General and Chancellor, Head of Archives, Bishop's House, Hove); the late Bernard Hurst; Ms Sandre Jackson (Archivist, Bishop's House, Hove); Wilf and Laura Jepson; Mrs Ann Joy; John and Mrs Ann Knox; John Leech; Mrs Valerie Ludlam; Mrs Isabelle McHardy; Mrs Marie-Thérèse Magee; Sister Margaret (St Martha's Convent, Rottingdean); Clive and Stephen Müdd; Mrs Eileen Noakes; Felicity O'Brien (Archbishop's secretary, Southwark Archdiocese); Peter O'Flinn; Sister Mary Patrice (St Martha's Convent, Falkirk); the late Sister Mary Pauline (St Martha's Convent, Rottingdean); Sister Pauline (St Martha's Convent, Rottingdean); Miss Bunty Phillips; Mrs Margaret Phillips, Arundel; Brother Bernard Philpott, Mayfield; John and Mrs Barbara Pierce; Mr and Mrs Sidney Pile; Michael Radford; Mrs Jean Rattrie; Mrs Rosemary Reade; Mrs Frances Reidy; John Remers; Brian Sheed, Head Teacher, Our Lady of Lourdes School ; Anne Shelley, St Joseph's College, Mill Hill; Mrs Violet Simpson; Brian and Margaret Slattery; Sister Marie-Christine, Lourdes, Brighton.

Mrs Alex Sloggett, Rottingdean Preservation Society; Edmund and Mrs Mary Smith; Mrs Phyllis Smith; Charles Snowden, *A and B News*; David and Mrs Alison Stainthorpe; Canon John Stapleton; Philip Stephens; Jim and Mrs Margie Sutton; Mrs Sally Sweeney; Mrs Brenda Taylor; Mrs Molly Taylor; Mrs Dana Towner; Mrs Mary Trimbey; Brian and Mrs Ann Turner; Bill and Mrs Pat Turner; Mrs Huguette Vincent; Mrs Janet Ward, Coventry; Syd Ward; Mrs Barbara Whatley; Mrs Jacqueline Wheatcroft, secretary of Our Lady of Lourdes School; Mrs Christine Whittington; Timothy Wilcox; Ken Wilkinson; Miss Ann Willis; Mrs Kathleen Willson; Mrs Geraldine Wilson; Mrs Sheila Woodman; Bernard Workman, Peter Wotton, Tonbridge; Mrs Dorothy Young.

Should anyone have been inadvertently omitted, I tender my sincere apologies and thank them for their assistance.

With regard to copyright and ownership of any source material, every endeavour was made to contact the parties concerned.

## PICTURE CREDITS

The author and publisher are most grateful to the *The Argus* for permission to use photographs of church occasions, which are individually credited. They also wish to thank the sisters of St Martha's Convent, Rottingdean Preservation Society, Our Lady of Lourdes School and the countless kind people who dug deep into their family and personal collections to supply pictures to illustrate this book.

# INDEX

Illustrations are indicated by page numbers in bold type